Awareness

Awareness is a popular topic with students of psychology because as humans we take pride in our awareness of the world around us and also the state of our inner mind, our feelings and our emotions. This accessible introductory text introduces the various states of awareness and consciousness, focusing mainly on sleeping, dreaming and the hypnotic state, but also examining the precise meanings of the terms 'consciousness' and 'awareness' and whether or not they are the same thing. Bodily rhythms are investigated in the light of recent research and the author shows how behaviour is affected when bodily rhythms are disturbed. Sleep and dreaming and their associated theories are explored, together with three theories of hypnosis. *Awareness* addresses the average student, making complex information accessible and straightforward.

Evie Bentley is Head of Psychology at Haywards Heath College. She has been active in establishing best practice in A-level Psychology teaching in the UK. She is current chair of the Association for the Teaching of Psychology.

Routledge Modular Psychology

Series editors: Cara Flanagan is the Assessor for the Associated Examining Board (AEB) and an experienced A-level author. Kevin Silber is Senior Lecturer in Psychology at Staffordshire University. Both are A-level examiners in the UK.

The *Routledge Modular Psychology* series is a completely new approach to introductory level psychology, tailor-made to the new modular style of teaching. Each short book covers a topic in more detail than any large textbook can, allowing teacher and student to select material exactly to suit any particular course or project.

The books have been written especially for those students new to higher-level study, whether at school, college or university. They include specially designed features to help with technique, such as a model essay at an average level with an examiner's comments to show how extra marks can be gained. The authors are all examiners and teachers at the introductory level.

The *Routledge Modular Psychology* texts are all user-friendly and accessible and include the following features:

- practice essays with specialist commentary to show how to achieve a higher grade
- chapter summaries to assist with revision
- progress and review exercises
- glossary of key terms
- summaries of key research
- further reading to stimulate ongoing study and research
- website addresses for additional information
- cross-referencing to other books in the series

Also available in this series (titles listed by syllabus section):

Awareness
Biorhythms, sleep and dreaming

Evie Bentley

London and New York

First published 2000
by Routledge
11 New Fetter Lane, London EC4P 4EE

Simultaneously published in the USA and Canada
by Routledge
29 West 35th Street, New York, NY 10001

Routledge is an imprint of the Taylor & Francis Group

Typeset in Times by Taylor & Francis Books Ltd
Printed and bound in Great Britain by Clays Ltd, St Ives plc

British Library Cataloguing in Publication Data
A catalogue record for this book is available from the British Library

Library of Congress Cataloging in Publication Data
Bentley, Evie, 1947–
Awareness: biorhythms, sleep, and dreaming / Evie Bentley
Includes bibliographical references and index.
1. Consciousness. 2. Awareness. 3. Biological rhythms.
4. Psychology, Comparative. I. Title.
BF311.B452   1999
154.4–dc21   99–30613

ISBN 0–415–18872–5 (hbk)
ISBN 0–415–18873–3 (pbk)

To Bill, Linnie and Hugh, VIPs indeed, with my love

Contents

Illustrations

Figures

Tables

Acknowledgements

Alison Corley, Assistant Librarian at St Anne's College, Oxford, for help in chasing references; Cara Flanagan for opportunity, encouragement and advice; my students for being willing and appreciative triallers; and the ATP, Pauline Dance, Matt Jarvis, Jill Keogh, Alison Kewley, Sue Loadsman, Deborah Patterson, Jon Rotheray, Pickles Vaid, Rosemary Walsh and the furred ones – Abi, Mollie and Tigger – for their support, encouragement and patience in many ways.

The series editors and Routledge acknowledge the expert help of Paul Humphreys, Examiner and Reviser for A-level Psychology, in compiling the Study Aids section of each book in the series.

They also acknowledge the Associated Examining Board (AEB) for granting permission to use their examination material. The AEB do not accept responsibility for the answers or examiner comment in the Study Aids section of this book or any other book in the series.

States of awareness and consciousness

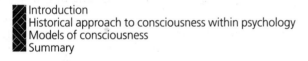

Introduction
Historical approach to consciousness within psychology
Models of consciousness
Summary

Introduction

This book is entitled *Awareness*. Why? Well, we humans have pride in our ability to be aware both of the world around us and of our inner mind. For instance, we are aware of our feelings and emotions. From the viewpoint of modern psychology there are several 'states' of awareness including sleep, dreaming, the hypnotic trance, lucid dreaming and even coma. This book focuses mainly on sleeping, dreaming and the hypnotic state, but there is on-going discussion as to the precise meanings of the terms 'consciousness' and 'awareness', and whether or not they mean the same thing. Even today psychologists are not able to agree on precise definitions. The concept of 'consciousness' has gone in and out of favour with psychologists, as we shall see.

Historical approach to consciousness within psychology

Wundt (1862) investigated consciousness using the now abandoned technique of **introspection**, training his participants to think deeply and describe their own mental images and feelings; their own thoughts really. He saw human consciousness as the fusing of external elements or stimuli, with internal elements such as personal emotions. This fusion produced what Wundt called our 'complexes of experience' which he saw as our consciousness. His explanations were based on his knowledge of chemistry: he thought of the external and internal elements of consciousness as mental atoms and the complexes of experience as molecules (for those of you who haven't done chemistry – molecules are arrangements of atoms).

James (1890) introduced the phrase 'streams of consciousness' to describe the constant internal mental 'noise' which we experience when awake. This stream was seen as the combined input from all our senses plus the resultant thoughts. James suggested that our awareness of the external world was due to this, but that we could focus that awareness in on certain aspects of the external or internal world. In other words we could channel our attention.

Introspection fell out of fashion with the advent of the behaviourists, such as Watson (1913) and Skinner (1938). Behaviourists argued that all behaviour could be explained in terms of learning theory and conditioning. For example, you learn that every time a bell is rung there will be food; eventually you salivate at the sound of the bell: you have learned a new association between a response (salivation) and a stimulus (the bell).

Behaviourists completely rejected the idea of consciousness because they felt it was a hypothetical and meaningless construct. They believed that consciousness was an epiphenomenon – a secondary effect which arises from brain activity but does not cause it. Consciousness was an unnecessary concept when explaining behaviour. Behaviourists similarly regarded concepts such as 'mind' and 'thought' as irrelevant to the scientific study of psychology. Such concepts had no use because they could not be observed directly nor measured.

At much the same time as James and then the behaviourists were working, a conflicting theory of consciousness was being devised by

Freud. This has developed into the psychodynamic approach and is described in detail later on in this chapter.

One final thought about consciousness concerns the question about whether non-human animals have consciousness. We need to distinguish being aware, which an animal might be, from being conscious, which an animal might not be. Dennett has suggested a good example. When a bee approaches a tree it is aware of the tree as an obstacle – it really could be anything that simply needs to be avoided – whereas we are aware (conscious) of the tree as a tree. The tree has meaning (an internal representation) that extends beyond mere avoidance of an obstacle.

Models of consciousness

Brain activity

One model of consciousness is based on brain activity, using **electro-encephalogram (EEG)** traces mainly. It is known that when a person is alert their EEG pattern is highly irregular, unsynchronised, with the spiky waves of electrical activity tightly massed together. When they are concentrating on something particular the trace changes. The waves become deeper vertically and more spread out horizontally, and they are described as slower waves. They also show a pattern called **theta waves** or rhythms. The same person in a relaxed and calm state has an EEG trace somewhere between the two described above. In a relaxed state their **brain waves** are faster than when concentrating and show an **alpha wave** rhythm. Figure 1.1 shows an EEG trace.

Another investigation of brain awareness or activity was done on epileptic patients who were having brain surgery to improve their condition (Penfield and Rasmussen, 1950). When operations were done on their brain the patients were awake while their skulls were opened and their brains exposed. The researchers obtained the patients' permission to stimulate areas of the brain using fine needle-like electrodes. As a result of these investigations, Penfield suggested that consciousness was located in the **thalamus** (part of the **forebrain**) and the upper part of the hindbrain.

Gazzaniga and Sperry (1967) took investigations into conscious-ness and brain functioning a stage further, also using patients treated surgically for epilepsy. These patients had their **corpus callosum** (a

3

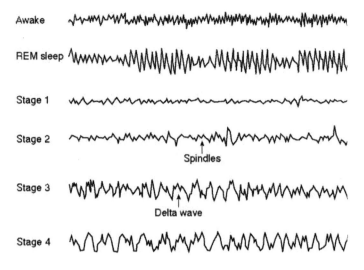

Figure 1.1 **Electro-encephalogram (EEG) trace from a relaxed person with eyes closed and then open**

group of nerve fibres which connect the two cerebral hemispheres) cut in a technique called **split-brain procedure**. These studies showed that the two halves of the brain (cerebral hemispheres) function independently of each other and have some separate functions, and also that they have some sort of independent consciousness. For example, one split-brain patient reported that when she had to decide what to wear, she sometimes found that her left hand picked out quite different clothes from those she had intended (Hayes, 1994). The suggestion is that the conscious decision was taken by the left hemisphere, but the hand reaching out was controlled by the right hemisphere (left hand controlled by right hemisphere). And of course the two hemispheres no longer communicated with each other. This may seem rather more science fiction than scientific psychology, and it does not demonstrate what or where consciousness actually is, but it does indicate that consciousness is complex and involves more than the hindbrain, and possibly involves communication between the left and right hemi-spheres.

Levels of consciousness

Some psychologists have suggested that there are three levels of consciousness: **conscious**, **pre-conscious** and **unconscious**.

The conscious mind is what we are aware of whilst awake. This is when we have self-awareness (see later section in this chapter) and so are aware of not just our environment but also our own thoughts and feelings, our sensations and responses. We also have self-control in this state and have free will to make choices and decisions. Maybe this includes our 'conscience', our ability to think morally and ethically.

The pre-conscious mind is thought of as on the fringes of the conscious mind. This is where we are not fully conscious of sensory input or thoughts, but we can focus down on them if this becomes desirable. The 'cocktail party phenomenon' (Cherry, 1953) is an example of this. At a cocktail (or other) party one might be busy with a group of people, apparently unaware of other people and what they are saying – until one's own name is spoken. At that point our atten-tion is immediately and vividly switched to that other group. Our pre-conscious mind had been monitoring other sensory input and has switched our attention. Sometimes the pre-conscious has been called the subconscious, but this term is more commonly used with Freudian connections and using the same term here might be confusing.

The unconscious mind is a construct of Freud (1901) and comprises the hypothesised mass of deeply repressed, disturbing memories and thoughts which control our behaviour and of which, since they are so repressed, we are unaware. Freud felt that much of this repressed unconscious was sexual in origin, maybe because he was living in sexually repressive times. His ideas have been developed into modern psychodynamic theory which largely agrees with Freud's interpretation of the unconscious. One exception is the modern school based on Jung, Freud's sometime follower, who believed that there was an additional and highly significant part of the unconscious – the **collective unconscious**. Jung hypothesised that this held the memories and feelings of all humanity, back through time. Jung was also less than sure about the sexual basis of the unconscious. However modern psychodynamic theory still supports the general principle, that is, the existence of a controlling unconscious made up of repressed emotions and memories.

Unfortunately, as this is so strongly repressed the unconscious cannot be accessed for study except in very non-empirical ways with individuals. There are therefore no real data to support or refute the existence of the unconscious and the psychoanalytic methods of investigating the unconscious have been criticised as being heavily dependent on the analyst, that is they are very subjective and are therefore prone to bias. Freud's own research has also been criticised as his samples were both very small and very biased – a few wives of fellow professionals plus one small boy – and Freud's own notes of his interviews with his sample were written afterwards, not at the time. This means that the generalisation of Freud's interpretations to the whole population could be challenged because his samples were not typical of the normal population. Also, we now know empirically that human memory is faulty and should not be relied upon as absolute truth and so there is the chance that Freud's recollections may not have been faultless. Then there is the point that Freud himself changed his own interpretation of his interviews, though this was from one subjective opinion to another. Nevertheless, Freud's theories undoubtedly made a great contribution to the way psychologists thought about human behaviour, in particular to the consideration of hidden motives and the conception of consciousness.

States of consciousness

The most obvious states of consciousness are being awake and being asleep. Psychological research has focused on sleep. There has also been considerable interest in whether or not the hypnotic state is a special state of consciousness.

The (non-Freudian) unconscious state

Victims of various accidents and unlucky sports people (such as boxers and horse riders) may become unconscious as a result of a blow to the head. In this state there is a complete lack of awareness of the external world and, as far as can be ascertained, also of much of their internal or mental world. In this state they cannot be woken up, they do not react to any stimuli, including pain, and EEG recordings show little brain activity. It really is as though the brain has 'gone down' to use a computer analogy – neurones have shut down, the 'closed' sign has gone up. It might be that this is a protective state, but not enough is known to make any certain conclusions. A similar state is caused by some anaesthetics and other drugs, and there are anec-dotal accounts of people who have appeared unconscious but have been able to report on what went on around them whilst in this state. We do not know yet whether we are dealing with one or several states with similar symptoms of being profoundly unaware.

Extreme examples of the unconscious state are when a person is in a **coma**. This is almost always the result of a brain injury. Coma is a sign of serious damage or disruption within the brain and if there is going to be recovery this is usually seen within a maximum of twenty weeks. People who are going to recover start to show small signs of reacting to external stimuli. Maybe their breathing-rate changes or the electrical conductivity of their skin alters or the heart-rate increases. Then they may be able to follow a moving object like a hand in front of their eyes. They may be able to make sounds and their sleep–wake cycle may restart. What happens depends on where the brain injury is and how bad it is.

If after about four months there is no improvement and brain scans show little neural activity in the forebrain, then the person may be said to be in a persistent vegetative state (PVS) (Jennet and Plum, 1972). This state is more likely to occur if the brain has at any time been severely short of oxygen for several minutes – irreversible damage begins after only three minutes unless the brain is very cold. People who have been trapped underwater or crushed underground can go into PVS and there is almost no chance at all of any improve-ment from this state of deep unconsciousness. Some people with PVS have lived for years and the occasional case reawakens completely unexpectedly, but mainly such unfortunate people slowly die. The body depends on the brain and if the brain is damaged badly enough the body cannot survive indefinitely.

Meditation

In the 1960s a single book (Tart, 1969) contained two-thirds of the research published in English on meditation. Yet now there are liter-ally thousands of such articles, showing the explosion of interest in this state of consciousness. The reason for this is probably because of the physiological applications of meditation to health and to coping with stress. EEG traces show that meditation is closely similar to very relaxed wakefulness and also to the hypnotic state. Meditation is at the core of **autogenic** and similar calming techniques, and of autohypnosis. All these states depend on the person being physically comfortable and then, by various ways, learning to switch off the **sympathetic** part of their **autonomic nervous system** and switch on the **parasympathetic** part. In this way they switch off the part which is keeping them physiologically tense and switch on their calming part.

A common way into this is by engaging in controlled, slow, deep breathing. This actually does alter brain waves and in this state people have been able to learn how to lower their high blood-pressure and dissipate or lower their anxiety levels to a bearable level. Some programmes also teach a relaxed-wakefulness form of meditation in which participants can observe their mental selves in a helpful and non-judgemental way which has been useful to both businesspeople needing to think more clearly and substance-abusers undergoing therapy (Engler in Clay, 1997).

Oakley's levels of awareness

Finally, one good attempt to give the controversial concept of consciousness some structure is Oakley's (1985) construct. He proposed three levels of awareness as follows:

Level 1   This refers to *simple awareness*, such as reflexes, and also to learning by classical conditioning (when a stimulus is associated with a new response as in the bell and salivation). This level of awareness would exist in simple nervous systems like the snail's. In animals with more complex nervous systems a certain amount of processing (simple awareness) takes place below the level of the cerebral hemispheres, for example spinal reflexes in mammals.

Level 2   This includes *consciousness* such as reasoning and memory, plus complex patterns of learning shown in the cortex and limbic system of advanced nervous systems. Some sorts of, for instance, foraging and homing behaviour would fit in here.

Level 3   This is *self-awareness*, that is an organism with a self-concept and self-image. Oakley suggested that this is only found in the primate group (humans and apes, that is mammals with the most highly evolved cortex), though not all researchers would agree with this. For example, some might include dolphins as a group of animals with self-awareness.

Oakley argued that consciousness requires a highly developed brain and that self-awareness requires an even more highly developed cortex. Currently much research is focused on information-processing within the brain and if this information-processing is sufficiently detailed then this model says that the creature has consciousness. But, according to Oakley's model, self-awareness would only occur when the processing is so detailed (requiring a very complex cortex) as to give the knowledge of self as separate and different from others.

Oakley's ideas are particularly interesting as they do not focus on language as the criterion for consciousness. His is a broader but also more clear approach and free from the confines of theories which state that without language there can be no consciousness at all.

Summary

Humans have been discussing the concept of 'consciousness' for centuries, and psychologists have continued the discussion into the present, with no agreement about the precise meaning of the term. Wundt and James were early psychologists who studied this concept using introspection. James introduced the term 'streams of consciousness'. In the early twentieth century, behaviourists such as Watson and Skinner rejected introspection and suggested that the concept of consciousness was irrelevant in psychology.

Various models of consciousness have been suggested. One approach is to record electrical activity in the brain (EEGs) using, for example, epileptic and split-brain patients. A different approach is to divide consciousness into levels: the conscious, pre-conscious and unconscious. The concept of the unconscious was introduced by Freud and this evolved into the modern psychodynamic approach. Jung, a post-Freudian, suggested a fourth level, the collective unconscious.

A third approach is to consider different states of awareness, such as coma and persistent vegetative state. Finally, Oakley produced a classification of different levels of awareness which could be used as a base from which to move forward.

Further reading

Zimbardo, P., McDermott, M., Jansz, J. and Metaal, N. (1995) *Psychology: A European text*. London: HarperCollins. (Pages 86–112 give an interesting view of this area of psychology.)

2

Bodily rhythms

Introduction
Circadian rhythms
Ultradian rhythms
Infradian rhythms
Circannual rhythms
Summary

Introduction

We live in a rhythmic world. Night follows day, the seasons on earth
and the stars above follow their annual patterns, lawn daisies close at
night and open in daylight, pubs open and pubs close! Behaviour too
follows **rhythms** whether or not we recognise them. Swallows migrate
to Sussex in June and depart down to Africa in September. Easter is
still associated with lambs and chicks, even though nowadays we can
manipulate breeding seasons so that lambs and chicks can be
produced all the year round. Nevertheless, the natural reproductive
rhythms of many non-human animals remain seasonal, so that the
newborn will appear when conditions are most favourable.

Rhythms of living things are called bodily rhythms or biorhythms.
These are patterns of physiological or psychological processes which
are repeated over periods of time. We both have them and are affected
by them. The main types of biorhythm can be grouped according to

their period or duration, that is how frequently they occur or how long they last, as:

Circadian   Around (*circa* means 'around') a day, that is 24 hours.
Ultradian   Less than a day, that is cycles which occur within a day such as meal-times.
Infradian   More than a day, including **circannual rhythms** (around a year).

Psychological research has focused on two aspects of biorhythms: what they are and what causes or controls them. In this chapter we will look at what psychologists have found out.

Circadian rhythms

These are rhythms with a cycle or period of about 24 hours. The most obvious one (and the most researched) is our own sleep–wake cycle. In any 24-hour period we go to sleep and wake up. The time spent in sleeping and waking varies from individual to individual and culture to culture. It also varies as you get older. We know that most babies sleep more than most adults and most elderly people sleep even less. The possible reasons behind these variations are discussed later in the different theories of sleep (see Chapter 5).

Most of the evidence, such as from Meddis (1975), shows an average of 7 to 8 hours sleep per 24 hours. We also know that there are some lucky individuals who thrive on very little sleep compared to the general population, a real example of **individual differences**. Records suggest that nowadays, at the turn of the twenty-first century, we are sleeping less by about one-and-a-half hours a night than did our forebears one hundred years ago at the turn of the twentieth century. Coren (1996) suggested that many of us are right now living in a state of mild **sleep deprivation**. We are not sleeping less because we need less sleep but because we now overrule natural daylight. We now make our environment as light as we want whatever the time of day or season, and so we keep awake longer and sleep less.

Studies of the sleep–wake cycle

Michel Siffre was studied for seven months in 1972 when he volunteered to live underground in caves out of any contact with daylight and without any other clues about what time of day it was, that is no watch or clocks or TV. He was safe and well fed, and the caves were warm and dry. He was always monitored via computers and video cameras, he had a 24-hour phone-link to the surface and was well catered for in mind and body with books and exercise equipment. In this isolated environment he quickly settled into a regular cycle of sleeping and waking. The surprise was that this cycle was of almost 25 hours, not 24! It was a very regular 24.9-hour rhythm, so that each 'day' he was waking up nearly an hour later. The effect of this was that by the end of his months underground he had 'lost' a considerable number of days and thought he had been underground for much less time than had actually passed.

This case study is a very clear demonstration of an **innate**, that is naturally occurring circadian rhythm in a human. In other words, the sleep–wake cycle is something we are born with and which is biologically determined. It functions in the absence of any external cues such as daylight. You might have thought that light and darkness are what make you feel tired and awake, but this study demonstrates that we go to sleep without such external cues. Such external cues are called *zeitgebers*, a German word which literally means 'time giver'.

One criticism of the Siffre study might be that it involved only one individual and perhaps we are not justified in concluding that *all* humans will behave in this way. However, the results have been confirmed by other cave studies (for example, Kleitman, 1963), as well as one which looked at a blind individual. Miles *et al.* (1977) described the case history of a young adult male, blind from birth, who had a strong 24.9-hour circadian rhythm. In spite of being able to hear a variety of possible time-cues or *zeitgebers* (such as clocks and radios), this young man was having considerable problems in resetting his personal circadian rhythm each day. In fact his problems were so great that he had to take stimulants in the mornings and sedatives at night in order to get his innate rhythm in time with the rest of the world.

However, not all studies have supported the 24.9-hour human sleep–wake rhythm. Folkard (1996) reported an interesting case study of a young woman, Kate Aldcroft, who was voluntarily isolated for 25 days without any *zeitgebers*. She shifted to a thirty-hour rhythm, and felt well and relaxed. The researchers used a novel method of marking her rhythms – they asked her to play 'Amazing Grace' on her bagpipes at what she felt were the same times, twice daily. There was a difference of hours in the actual times when she in fact played the song. Folkard reported that the participant had slept for up to 16 hours at a time and suggested that, though her temperature rhythm was a 24-hour one, her sleep rhythm might be on a 30-hour cycle.

Progress exercise

Of course, this participant was a university student and her lifestyle and sleep–wake rhythm before the study might have included factors with a lasting knock-on effect. Suggest two factors in her life before the study which could have influenced her behaviour during the study.

One final note about the sleep–wake cycle. One might ask – why 24.9 hours (if that *is* our innate rhythm)? One suggestion is that, in the very distant past, the earth might have had a longer rotation cycle so that our days were more like 25 hours. So maybe our internal clock is set to this rhythm and is yet to adapt. However, the fact is that the earth used to spin faster.

Studies of other circadian rhythms

There is also a 24-hour cycle in **metabolic rate** – the personal or cellular rate of energy-use. Colquhuon (1970) found that humans had a metabolic rhythm which peaked at about 4 p.m. and dipped 12 hours later, at 4 a.m. This rhythm correlated with many cognitive functions, such as memory and attention. Interestingly there was also a small post-lunch dip, which could be explained from the action of the autonomic nervous system (ANS) and digestive system. The ANS is a discrete group of nerves which have control of many involuntary or *automatic* (thus 'autonomic') activities, such as heartbeat and blood pressure: we don't have to think about them consciously, they occur automatically. The ANS is divided into the sympathetic and parasympathetic nervous systems. The latter has the effect of slowing us down after we have eaten so that the body's resources can concentrate on processing the food rather than being used elsewhere – the function of the parasympathetic system is sometimes called 'rest and digest'. So it would make sense that, after eating a meal, there would be a dip in our metabolic rate (the post-lunch dip).

Unfortunately for this simple explanation this dip in the cognitive cycle seems to happen regardless of meals, so currently there is no good rationale for its existence. Folkard (1983) suggested that the cognitive cycle is the result of a special autonomic arousal rhythm. In other words he is seeing the circadian cognitive cycle as a side-effect of the ANS cycle, so that when the ANS slows us down to rest-and-digest, other functions such as mental and cognitive arousal also reduce. Perhaps we should all alter our behaviour and have lunch followed by a siesta so we are in harmony with this innate rhythm – research suggests our cognitive performance would benefit!

Body core temperature also varies on a 24-hour rhythm because heat is a by-product of metabolism – that is, it is a by-product of any energy turnover or use. This is why, when you are using more energy (for instance, in playing sport or running for a bus), you feel hotter. So the production of body heat follows the metabolic rhythm and peaks at 4 p.m. and dips at 4 a.m. This rhythm is well known, but evidence for it being an innate rhythm was demonstrated by Bollani *et al.*'s (1997) study of babies in the first two days of life. The researchers monitored the babies' core temperature every ten minutes for up to two days, by which time all six babies were showing a clear 24-hour main rhythm, temperature-wise. This was presumed to be due to an innate mechanism because, in that time, it was unlikely that the infants would be responding to *zeitgebers*.

Ultradian rhythms

These operate in cycles of less than 24 hours, that is they happen more than once a day. The Bollani *et al.* study also showed up shallow ultradian temperature fluctuations in many of the babies studied, in other words their temperature had a rise and dip (though the changes were small) more than once a day. A study by Klein and Armitage (1979) found ultradian rhythms in **cognitive vigilance**, namely a 96-minute cycle in participants' performance on verbal and spatial tasks. They called this the 'basic rest–activity cycles' (BRAC) and suggested that it might be related to rhythms during sleep. According to Carlson (1986) there are actually numerous cycles all with a periodicity of approximately 90 minutes and all linked to a controlling mechanism, a biological clock, in the medulla. This 'clock' seems to control a pattern of regular changes in our alertness and associated activity during the day, as well as the NREM and REM sleep cycles at night.

Sleep stages

The clearest example of ultradian rhythms comes from the study of sleep cycles, which is looked at more closely in Chapter 4. The data are largely from a classic study by Dement and Kleitmen (1957) conducted on nine sleeping participants for up to 61 nights in a laboratory. They all showed quite considerable similarity in their sleep cycles, the rhythms which occurred during sleep. Dement and Kleitman found two distinct kinds of sleep: periods when the eyes moved rapidly under closed eyelids (rapid eye movement or REM sleep) and times when the eyes were motionless (NREM sleep). These sleep periods alternated during the sleep period. There was an observed rhythm in this alternation, starting with NREM sleep and varying between individuals but reasonably constant for any one participant. The mean was a 92-minute NREM and REM rhythm. There is more about this key study in Chapter 9.

When participants were woken from REM sleep, dreams were recalled 152 times and no dreams reported 39 times, that is dreaming was reported over 79 per cent of the time. When woken from NREM sleep, dream recall fell to under 7 per cent (11 out of 160 times). Therefore the ultradian rhythm is one of alternately NREM and REM sleep, with the latter being associated with dreaming though not exclusively so.

Infradian rhythms

These have cycles of longer than 24 hours. Examples include the human **menstrual cycle**, which is more or less monthly, and the reproductive cycle in cats and dogs, which occurs twice a year. There have also been suggestions of various interesting lunar effects. For example, is there a real link between mental disorders and the moon, or was the idea of a 'lunatic' merely superstition? Research may eventually be able to tell us. Nevertheless, there are many confirmed instances of behaviour that is related to the moon. For instance, seashore crabs move up and down their territory in time with the tides (caused by the moon's gravitational pull on the earth's waters) even if they are kept in constant laboratory conditions (Palmer, 1989). There is also the Pacific Palolo worm, as reported by Roberts (1982: 393), which rises to the ocean surface – turning it white – just once a year at dawn, precisely one week after the November full moon. This could well be evidence of a lunar-influenced innate neural clock.

The human menstrual cycle

Human menstruation is the best-researched infradian rhythm. This cycle is innate in females of reproductive age, regardless of culture. It is an example of a biorhythm which is controlled by **hormones** – biochemical messengers which are synthesised by glands of the **endocrine system**. Hormones are released into the blood and travel in the bloodstream to their target organs – their sites of action (see Kevin Silber's *The Physiological Basis of Behaviour*, in this series, for a fuller account). In the case of the menstrual cycle the hormones are oestrogen and progesterone (**ovarian hormones**) and the target organs are the ovaries and womb.

There are clear individual variations in the length of this rhythm or cycle, but the average seems to be about 28 days. This does not mean a cycle of different length is unusual or abnormal. It is not unknown to find a range of menstrual cycles from, say, 20 days to 60 days. The menstrual cycle starts with the ripening of an egg and the thickening of the lining of the womb, ready to receive a fertilised egg. Each cycle ends with the menstrual bleeding, or menstruation, unless pregnancy occurs. The purpose of the cycle is to prepare the womb for the possibility of pregnancy, so a fertilised ovum can successfully grow and be nourished. The hormone oestrogen prepares the lining of the womb for this, then the hormone progesterone maintains the womb-lining for a few days. Then, if there is no pregnancy, the lining is shed as menstruation. If there is a pregnancy, the womb will be freshly prepared to support the pregnancy. The lining continues to grow and form the placenta which will nourish the embryo.

17

It has been observed that communities of women, such as girls in boarding schools or women's colleges and nuns, all seem to have their menstrual cycles synchronised. It may be that the biorhythms of women who spend time together are controlled by **pheromones**, odourless chemicals released involuntarily by individuals and transported by the air, which carry messages within a species from one individual to another.

This has been demonstrated empirically by Russell *et al.* (1980). They collected sweat every day from one woman (the donor). This was then dissolved in alcohol to kill any bacteria and wipes of this mixture were applied under the noses of their female participants, also on a daily basis. The participants' menstrual cycles soon became synchronised with the donor's, showing a clear effect.

It is thought the natural and odourless pheromone molecules dissolve inside the nose and stimulate neurones which in turn affect the hypothalamus and alter the pattern of hormone production. Why this should happen is not certain, though one suggestion might be as follows. We humans are social animals and live in social groups. We think this would also have been true of our remote ancestors. It would probably have been a real advantage for a social group to have synchronised pregnancies, which would result in several mothers breastfeeding at the same time. This would not only mean that if a mother was ill or died another could take over feeding the baby, but that the mothers could in effect work shifts. Some could go and gather and prepare food and do other tasks, whilst others could feed the babies. So this synchronisation-by-proximity could make good sense in evolutionary terms. It is certainly seen in other non-human species, for instance in African lions, where lionesses in a pride operate on just such a system.

Circannual rhythms

These rhythms have a periodicity of about one year, that is they are annual rhythms. They are also infradian. **SAD (seasonal affective disorder)** could be considered one such rhythm – it describes people who become seriously depressed each autumn and feel better in late spring. **Migrations** and **hibernation** are other examples.

Name three animals which hibernate and, for one of your examples, suggest why this circannual behaviour is an advantage to it.

SAD and neurotransmitter systems

Some brain **neurotransmitters** have seasonal variations which may be circannual. Our nervous system has a large number of different neurotransmitters, some within the brain and some in the nerves. They are all chemicals which act on **neurones** (or nerve cells), usually at the junctions between neurones called **synapses**. Neurotransmitters cross these synaptic junctions to alter the likelihood of **nerve impulses** occurring in the next neurone. Some facilitate or make it easier for new impulses to be generated and others inhibit or make it more difficult for the new impulses to start. Production of **melatonin**, a hormone and neurotransmitter produced by the **pineal gland** in the forebrain, varies with the quantity of natural light, that is its concentration varies with the seasons. People who are particularly sensitive to their circulating levels of melatonin can suffer in winter from a low-melatonin type of depression called seasonal affective disorder or SAD, which is discussed further in Chapter 7.

Migration

Swallows fly north from Africa or southern Europe to Britain late each spring, as shown in Figure 2.1. It has been suggested that the factors affecting such migrations could be either food supplies or day-length. These are possible external triggers or *zeitgebers*. However, this would suggest that the birds are highly sensitive to relatively small changes in ambient temperature, day-length, light intensity, food availability or other seasonal variations, because tropical regions do not have much in the way of such changes. It isn't clear what triggers this northerly migration from around the equator but, on the other hand, we can explain the annual migrations south using the seasonal factors because there are very clear differences in food supplies and day-length.

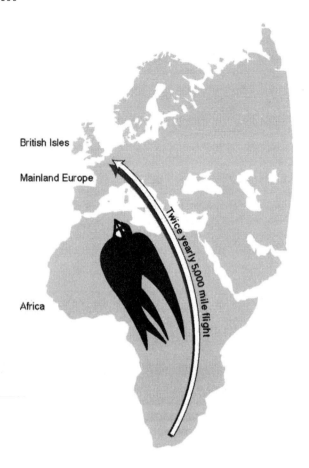

Figure 2.1 **The migration rhythm followed by swallows twice a year**

We can also explain the annual migrations of starlings from north-east Europe to southern England and that of Canada geese from the arctic to northern Britain because again there are distinct seasonal variations in light, temperature and so on as triggers for the behaviour patterns. We can hypothesise that changes in light or temperature, both of which decrease in autumn and increase in spring, stimulate a brain centre and trigger the migratory behaviour. In autumn the behaviour pattern would be to migrate in a direction towards warmer regions with more daylight; in spring the behaviour would be the reverse and the animals would move to less warm and less bright regions. It could be suggested that these migrations are genetically inherited, nature rather than nurture.

Hibernation

The greatest amount of research has however been done on a north American squirrel, the gold-mantled ground squirrel found in the Rocky Mountains. First reported by Pengelly and Fisher (1957), these squirrels naturally start the hibernating process in late autumn: they become less active and seek a suitable location within their burrows in which to hibernate. Then their level of physiological arousal falls and with it their body temperature also falls from the mammalian norm of about 37°C down to 1°C. In this state they can survive for months with no food and in very low ambient temperatures. They do not even need to breathe very often, as when the body is at this low temperature it needs almost no oxygen and food. The reverse happens in spring, with hibernation ending in April.

These rhythmic changes were observed in a squirrel kept in laboratory conditions at a constant temperature and with 12 hours of light alternating with 12 hours of darkness. In their natural environment, the researchers suggested, it is unlikely that day-length would be an environmental trigger because the squirrels spend so much time in their burrows. However temperature might be a *zeitgeber*. In the experiment the squirrels still hibernated, suggesting (since temperature was controlled) that these squirrels did have a brain mechanism or **biological clock** which told them when to hibernate. It is rather difficult otherwise to see what would set off these changes in behaviour.

Make a large table for yourself as a summary of this chapter. Have one row for each type of rhythm and label the vertical divisions as follows:

Definition	Example	Main evidence (e.g. names of researchers + date)	Supporting evidence

Hint: Use a piece of file paper on its side as this will make constructing the table easier.

Summary

Our world is a rhythmic one and we divide up the rhythms into three groups: circadian (around a day), ultradian (less than a day) and infradian (more than a day).

The sleep–wake cycle is the main example of a circadian rhythm, with cognitive, autonomic and metabolic cycles also studied. Cave studies show an innate 24.9-hour cycle, but not all studies support this.

Body temperature is an example of an ultradian rhythm, as is cognitive vigilance and brain arousal. The main example of a human ultradian rhythm is however linked to sleep and is the alternation between quiet non-dreaming (NREM) sleep and dreaming (REM) sleep.

The obvious human example of an infradian rhythm is the menstrual cycle, controlled by hormones and pheromones. Females living in communities tend to have synchronised cycles, possibly an evolutionary aspect of our behaviour. Circannual rhythms are a special type of infradian rhythm with a duration of about a year. Hibernation, migration and SAD (seasonal affective disorder) are examples.

Further reading

Silber, K. (1999) *The Physiological Basis of Behaviour: Neural and hormonal processes*. London and New York: Routledge. (This book explains the basic details of brain structure, which is useful for understanding many of the structures mentioned in this book.)

www.sciencenet.org.uk (This is a science resource site with an interesting psychology section, including brain topics.)

Control of
biorhythms

Introduction

It is abundantly clear that biorhythms exist, in ourselves, non-human animals and even plants. This leads us to ask the main question – how they are controlled? Do we contain some sort of biological, **internal clock** and, if so, where is it? Or are we unconsciously sensitive to external, environmental cues (*zeitgebers*) which switch behaviours on and off? As we shall see, there is evidence for both internal and external clocks, and we have been able to identify the physiological mechanisms tied in with our internal clocks.

Evidence for internal clocks

An internal or **endogenous** clock (or set of clocks) is proposed as some sort of biological mechanism that sets a pace. Such a biological clock would be innate – but then so are many *zeitgebers*: our response to lightness is automatic and innate. Biological clocks are innate and internal, set by biological mechanisms. Their 'tick' may be a 24-hour one (as for the sleep–wake cycle), an 8-hour one (as in the rhythms of sleep) or even a 12-month one (as in patterns of hibernation).

Studies on humans

The Michel Siffre study mentioned in Chapter 2 is definite support for the existence of an endogenous (that is, an innate) clock. He was underground, with no natural light to tell him if it were day or night. He had videos to watch, but not television, as that would have identified what time it was. He had all sorts of activities and facilities but no clock or watch and nothing which could serve as or give him any *zeitgeber* (cue from outside his body). Yet he settled quickly and well into a circadian rhythm which was approximately a 25-hour cycle, not the 24-hour cycle you might have expected.

The study by Miles *et al.* (1977) based on a blind man and another by Aschoff (1965) which involved several participants living in a cave together, all confirm this approximate 25-hour rhythm when there are no external *zeitgebers* to indicate time of day or night. Therefore it must be that sleep–wake cycles are purely governed by internal, physiological cues.

Non-human animal studies

Non-human animal studies also support the existence of an endogenous clock. Rae Silver and her team (cited in Blakemore, 1988a) have conducted research on endogenous clocks in pigeons and in hamsters. They knew that pigeon pairs share the incubation of eggs in the nest by taking turns at sitting and they demonstrated that these turns are controlled by internal clocks, fixed in a pattern of 6-hour shifts. If one bird was delayed by, say, 2 hours in returning to take over in the nest (for example arriving at 3 p.m. instead of 1 p.m.) it would not leave after 4 hours, that is at 7 p.m. which would have been the 'right' time for handing over *if* the bird was using an external cue. The bird would only leave after it had been sitting for 6 hours (that is at 9 p.m.), even though the partner bird was waiting to take over. This rhythm was clearly not controlled by *zeitgebers* but must be determined by some internal mechanism, an extra clock perhaps, switched on by the start of the incubation shift. I say 'extra' because this would be a clock which is *additional* to the sleep–wake cycle clock.

Internal clocks and the brain

Evidence from studies of birds suggests that the sleep–wake cycle clock may be located in the pineal gland. In chickens a pair of pineal glands lie at the upper surface of the brain, just under the thin top of the skull, as shown in Figure 3.1. Binkley (1979) showed that the glands contain light receptors. Some of the light falling on the top of the head penetrates the thin skull and stimulates the pineal gland, as shown in Figure 3.1. It is known that the pineal gland secretes the hormone melatonin in inverse proportion to the amount of light falling on the bird: as light decreases melatonin increases. This would mean that at dusk the production of melatonin is increased and the reverse happens at dawn. Increased melatonin is associated with sleep – so we can see how changes in light can trigger an internal mechanism which governs the sleep–wake cycle. This explains why chickens become active at daybreak (also known as cock-crow!) and also would adjust the birds' activity to fit in with the seasonal variations in day-length.

Experiments on hamsters have demonstrated how the internal clock may work in mammals as distinct from birds. If a tiny region of the forebrain called the **SCN (supra-chiasmatic nucleus)** was removed then the hamsters' nocturnal behaviour (that is their circadian rhythm) disappeared. However, it was re-established if fetal SCN cells were subsequently implanted and allowed to grow. The fetal cells presumably took over the function of the lost SCN neurones. Other research on hamsters involved transplanting SCNs from mutant animals with a different circadian rhythm into non-mutant animals; the recipients quickly changed their rhythm to that of the donor, mutant, SCN (Morgan, 1995).

In addition, experiments with rats, who have shown a 25-hour circadian rhythm like humans, have linked damage to the SCN with complete disappearance of the circadian rhythm.

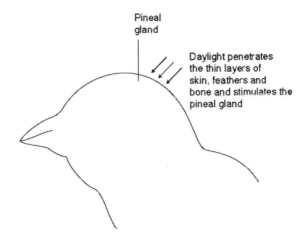

Pineal
gland

Daylight penetrates
the thin layers of
skin, feathers and
bone and stimulates the
pineal gland

Figure 3.1 **The position of the pineal gland in birds**

Human internal clocks

We too have an SCN. It is significant that a tiny nerve branches off the optic nerve from each eye and goes up to this tiny group of neurones (nerve cells). Whatever the amount and quality of light entering the eye, this light will generate nerve impulses which will travel out of the eye, along the optic nerve and into the brain. Some of these impulses will go along the nerve branch to the SCN, taking along the information about the light, as shown in Figure 3.2.

We know that the SCN is thus informed of the level of natural light. In this way the variations and cycle of natural light can influence these special SCN neurones which have an innate circadian **rhythmic firing pattern**.

The next stage of the process of biorhythm control now involves the pineal gland. The SCN neurones regulate the pineal gland and its production of melatonin in the following way. If you recall, in lower animals (for example, birds) light directly affected the pineal gland. In humans the pineal gland is triggered into action by the SCN (which was triggered by light from the retina) and then produces melatonin, which builds up from dusk. A critical level of melatonin influences

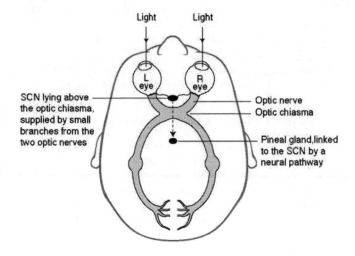

Figure 3.2 **The visual pathway in the brain showing the connection to the supra-chiasmatic nucleus (SCN) and onward to the pineal gland**

sleep, that is we feel the need to fall asleep when there is enough mela-tonin circulating in the blood.

So it seems that we have at least two endogenous mechanisms, the SCN and the pineal gland, which work together to control our circa-dian rhythm.

A second endogenous clock

We have behavioural and physiological evidence to support the exis-tence of one endogenous clock – but another clock seems to exist as well. When people living in caves modify their sleep–wake rhythm to suit themselves, as opposed to relying on light and darkness, their circadian rhythms altered to fit the new sleep–wake times with the exception of body temperature! This suggests a separate time-clock for the temperature cycle (Hawkins and Armstrong-Esther, 1978). In

Chapter 2 we saw that body temperature follows a circadian rhythm with a peak at 4 p.m. and a trough 12 hours later.

There is also the 90–96 minute cycle, found in both our REM/NREM sleep rhythm and in our cognitive vigilance during the day, which suggests another internal 'clock' or pacemaker (Klein and Armitage, 1979). This cycle was also described in Chapter 2.

Evidence for environmental influence (*zeitgebers*)

So are biological clocks all there is to control our biorhythms? Far from it. We know that various environmental cues can affect and reset our internal biological clocks. Why do we feel so ghastly when we have travelled across several time-zones? Why do most of us find it difficult to work shifts, especially if these shifts change from week to week? Well, the answer to these questions seems to lie in our sensitivity to *zeitgebers* – environmental cues.

Resetting the clocks

We have to be sensitive to our environment. It's essential for survival not only in the wild but also in our 'civilised' lives. For instance, if we did not alter our clothing to suit the environment we would easily succumb to hyper- or hypothermia, not to mention feeling uncomfortable and looking silly. In the wild, animals need to respond to seasonal variations by shedding hair or travelling to warmer climates. We also learn to associate points in our circadian rhythm with environmental cues such as mealtimes, coffee-breaks and time-for-bed. We learn to feel hungry at certain times of day. This could explain why stomachs seem to rumble more just before mealtimes than when we are not expecting food.

Light as a zeitgeber

This environmental awareness extends to having an *innate* response to both the amount and quality of light, as described above. Psychologists believe that *zeitgebers* can and do reset our endogenous clocks on at least a daily basis, so that we adapt to 24-hour cycles in a 24-hour world even though we contain a 25-hour innate clock. This means that when we wake up in the morning our brain clocks are reset by morning light and our brains get ready for another day. So the morning light which resets the chickens' pineal glands (mentioned earlier in this chapter) is a *zeitgeber* for them too. In fact light is a *zeitgeber* for most animals – remember those Palolo worms mentioned in Chapter 2 who respond to the November full moon. Maybe this might be a factor in explaining why many of us find it so much more difficult to get up in winter, when it's darker until later in the morning – the quality of light is simply not high enough to reset our internal clock up to wakefulness!

Biochemicals as zeitgebers

We have seen how pheromones may reset the human menstrual cycle (Colquhuon, 1970 – see Chapter 2) and thus are acting as *zeitgebers*. A further interesting fact about how external factors may affect menstrual cycles is that women who work with men tend to have shorter menstrual cycles. This suggests that *male* pheromones may also be acting as *zeitgebers* for the female reproductive bio-clock (McClintock, 1971). This could be explained in evolutionary terms: females who reproduce more often will have more offspring and therefore their genetic line is likely to become dominant. Therefore it is adaptive for females to ovulate more often when men are about, leading to shorter menstrual cycles.

Conclusion

There's more about *zeitgebers* in Chapter 7, but one of the most telling pieces of evidence about them is that in their complete absence (for example, when people live underground), the normal circadian rhythm alters and becomes unsynchronised with the 24-hour rhythm of the world in which we live. This supports the view that environmental cues have a 'stronger' effect and, as we noted at the start of this section, it is for good reason – we need to respond to our environment to survive.

Physiological control of biorhythms

The research described earlier in this chapter about the SCN and its links to the pineal gland are the key to the physiological control of the sleep–wake clock – both for the internal and external mechanisms. In this section we will look in more detail at the physiological processes.

Exogenous (external) control

It seems that morning light is received by the light-sensitive cells in the eye, the rods and cones, and stimulates nerve impulses which travel in the two optic nerves. Some impulses travel along a tiny branch off the optic nerves and reach and reset the SCN. This SCN also communicates with the pineal gland, further back in the forebrain. Increased levels of light cause the pineal gland to cease producing melatonin. But from dusk the low levels of light detected in the SCN stimulate the pineal gland to produce melatonin again. As the melatonin accumulates it influences production of **serotonin**, a brain neurotransmitter involved in many pathways including mood and sleep. This serotonin accumulates in the **raphe nuclei** in the hindbrain, near the **pons**, and stimulates the shutting down of the **RAS (reticular activating system)** which is closely linked with brain activity. So serotonin could be the switch to start the sleep clock and the suggested sequence might be as illustrated in Figure 3.3.

Endogenous (internal) control

Jouvet (1967) also suggested that another region, the **locus coeruleus** in the pons, used a different neurotransmitter, noradrenaline. In his experiments, if this area was damaged, noradrenaline levels fell and REM sleep was impaired. He proposed that each area plus its neurotransmitter controls one type of sleep – the raphe nuclei and its serotonin pathway controls NREM sleep, the locus coeruleus and **noradrenaline pathway** control REM sleep (see Figure 3.4). He also hypothesised a link between the two systems so that the two types of

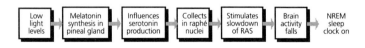

Figure 3.3 **Summary of the brain mechanism involved in sleep**

sleep alternate. More recent research has started to understand the complicated circuitry involved (for example, Sakai, 1985). It would appear that this circuitry involves the pons, raphe nuclei and locus coeruleus (among others) and involves a number of different neuro-transmitters, especially serotonin, noradrenaline and acetylcholine.

Supporting evidence comes from links to other brain areas. The locus coeruleus has a pathway to the **cerebellum**, an area known to control eye movements and muscle coordination – perhaps this is how the eye movements of REM are effected. The raphe nuclei have a pathway to the hypothalamus, which also controls body temperature and growth and repair. And electrical stimulation of a neighbouring group of cells to the locus coeruleus brings about REM-style paralysis.

Unfortunately, this nice model falls down as Ramm's (1979) review of relevant research shows no ill effects on REM sleep from damage to the locus coeruleus or its pathways, though there is good evidence for the role of the raphe nuclei and their pathways on NREM sleep. Stern and Morgane (1974) suggest that REM sleep is really needed for the resynthesis of neurotransmitters, particularly noradrenaline and

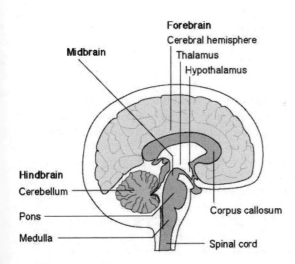

Figure 3.4 **The main regions of the human brain**

dopamine, and this does fit in with the known effect of tricyclic and other antidepressants which reduce REM sleep and increase noradrenaline levels.

In conclusion

Evidence for biological clocks comes from even the simplest organisms. For instance, single-celled algae from the intertidal zone burrow up to the sand surface as the tide ebbs and go back under the sand again as the tide flows in, so that they can photosynthesise without being washed away. Evolutionary biopsychology is now suggesting that these biological clocks started as single, light-sensitive molecules in primitive bacteria and have evolved into current, complex structures (as reported by Highfield, 1996).

Our own main internal clock having a 25- not 24-hour rhythm can also be interpreted from an evolutionary perspective. Being able to adapt is critical for biological success and our species is immensely adaptable as our varied cultures and habitats show. By having the potential to adjust our day/night clock to suit the local conditions and being able to alter the relative timings of our own rhythms, we are successfully adapting to our environment so we fit in and live in tune with it, and work with not against it. And, as you will see from Chapter 7, this also makes us happier.

Summary

Biorhythms exist and it is only sensible to assume that they are controlled by some sort of 'clock', an endogenous (internal) clock in the brain. Evidence for endogenous clocks comes from both human and non-human animal studies. Humans have been studied in the absence of light – either underground or involving blind participants. Pigeons and rats are some of the animals used.

The main brain-clock is likely to be the SCN (supra-chiasmatic nucleus) which has neural connections to the eyes and thus obtains information about light-levels. The SCN is also linked to the pineal gland which produces melatonin when dusk falls. This in turn is linked to serotonin secretion which has an effect on neural sleep-pathways. There is at least one other endogenous clock controlling the body-temperature rhythm.

Exogenous (external) factors also affect the setting of the clocks. These *zeitgebers* include light and pheromones.

Further reading

Green, S. (1998) Sleeping. *Psychology Review* 4 (3), February, 23–6. (An interesting and useful overview of the psychology of sleep.)
Gribbin, M. (1990) All in a night's sleep. *New Scientist: Inside Science* 36, 7 July, http://www.newscientist.com/ (This has accounts of research into biochemical factors involved with sleep.)
bisleep.medsch.ucla.edu/ (This has a home page with links to various information sources on the brain.)

4

Investigating sleep
The most obvious rhythm

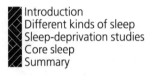

Introduction

The essential need for sleep in order to behave and feel 'normal' is known across cultures and time. A mediæval man in England who had served the years of preparation as a squire to become knighted had to spend the night before the final ceremony kneeling, awake, in vigil to prove himself able for the honour and duty of a knight. And today where people wish to demonstrate their strong feelings in peaceful protest, the all-night vigil is often used. It is a sign of how deeply people feel that they are willing to give up their sleep. Less happily, sleep deprivation has been and is used as part of brain-washing techniques by authorities all over the world.

On a different level we are probably all too familiar with the mentally dull feelings after a very late night, especially if this has been followed by an early class! A sleep deficit has well-known effects and many people also believe we can suffer from similar mental dullness after a surfeit of sleep. But is there any empirical evidence as to the effects of sleep disturbances? Many studies have been done on both non-human animals and our own species. Before we look at these we will consider the extent to which sleep is both an circadian and ultradian rhythm.

Different kinds of sleep

Sleep is an altered state of consciousness but not a state of unconsciousness – even the deepest sleeper can be woken up, though this can sometimes take quite a bit of doing! We go to sleep once a day and within this period of sleep we experience a number of different states of consciousness. Dement and Kleitman's research, described in Chapter 2, showed not only two types of sleep with associated brain wave (EEG) patterns, but also that the two types alternate in an ultradian rhythm and that dreaming is associated much more strongly with one of those types.

The two types of sleep are rapid eye movement or REM sleep and non-rapid eye movement or NREM sleep, and Dement and Kleitman found that waking participants during REM sleep was usually accompanied by a report of dreaming whereas waking out of NREM was far less likely to produce such reports. Therefore it is a mistake to equate REM sleep with dreaming but there is a strong association.

Stages of sleep

Further research has shown that we go through four separate stages of NREM as we fall asleep. Participants who have volunteered to sleep in various sleep-research laboratories have been wired up to computers and recorders. This is usually done for several nights in succession, so that participants can get used to the artificial conditions and start sleeping more naturally. Studies have shown that after the first night, when the arrangement of sleeping is strange, participants do sleep normally (Empson, 1989). In such studies tiny metal discs called electrodes are taped to the skin at points on the head and wires from these discs or electrodes connect to the computer. Any tiny electrical changes from the brain are picked up by these electrodes and passed to the computers. These changes are then shown graphically as an electro-encephalogram or EEG trace and the patterns produced are also called brain waves. See also Figure 1.1, page 4.

Stages of NREM sleep

Each stage of sleep has its own corresponding EEG patterns and this is what has given us the knowledge that there are four stages in NREM sleep (which is also known as **quiet sleep**).

When we are awake and *active* our brain rhythms are busy and this shows as a pattern of rapid and irregular brain waves – the EEG traces show very many, tightly packed, unsynchronised brain waves called beta waves. When we are awake and *relaxed* we see the presence of rhythmic waves called alpha waves in the brain EEG.

Stage 1 NREM

Stage 1 sleep is when we are falling asleep and takes up to 15 minutes. Recordings show brain waves slowing down from the slow alpha waves of relaxation to even slower and more irregular theta waves (see Figure 1.1). These patterns become synchronised, that is a regular pattern emerges. The parasympathetic nervous system is active ('rest and digest') and so heart-rate slows and muscles relax. This is when we may not be aware that we are falling asleep and this state is quite similar to that of deep relaxation or meditation. It is easy to be wakened from this state and we can also jolt back into full consciousness, often thinking that something significant has happened – like the phone ringing – when in fact it hasn't. This relaxed first stage of sleep is also known as the **hypnogogic state**, and **hallucinatory images** (meaning perceptual experiences which seem very real but which in fact are illusions) occurring here are linked to creativity.

Stage 2 NREM

Stage 2 lasts about 20 minutes and is when the brain waves get slower and larger with intermittent little bursts of activity called **sleep spindles**, electrical activity which is still understood in terms of its purpose or function. There are also k-complexes, which are tiny bursts of activity associated with external stimuli that do not awaken us, such as the wind whistling outside your window. Heart-rate, blood pressure and body temperature continue to fall and quiet sounds no longer waken us.

Stage 3 NREM

Stage 3 has further falls in heart- and breathing-rate and brain waves slow still more into delta waves. It's now quite difficult to be woken. This stage, like the previous ones, lasts for only a few minutes.

Stage 4 NREM

Stage 4 is the deepest sleep. Metabolic rate is at its lowest and it is very difficult to waken out of this state – unless there is a personally significant noise such as your own baby crying. Brain waves are at their slowest too. This stage lasts typically for 30–40 minutes and is the bottom of the 'sleep staircase'. Though it is the deepest stage of quiet sleep this is the stage where sleepwalking is more likely to occur, which seems odd, and not necessarily connected with dreaming (Jacobson and Kales, 1967). Sleep-talking also occurs in deep NREM sleep, although this can also happen – less often – during REM sleep (Arkin *et al.*, 1970).

REM sleep

After half an hour or so in Stage 4 sleep, suddenly the EEG trace speeds up the 'sleep staircase' through Stages 3 and 2, showing the brain is suddenly more active. The brain waves desynchronise and become complex as well as faster, and the brain's oxygen- and glucose-demands increase. The eyes start to move under closed eyelids, we go into REM or dreaming sleep and are most difficult to wake.

Though we are now cerebrally very active we are physically inactive, our bodies are almost as if paralysed. The reticular formation or RAS in the mid-brain seems to set up a block, isolating the brain from the rest of the body. Only the heart and lungs seem to match the speeding up of the brain. This REM sleep lasts for only about 10–15 minutes and completes the first sleep cycle of the night.

We then go back down through Stages 2 to 4 again and this cycle repeats about every 90 minutes through the night, though the time spent in Stages 3 and 4 gets progressively less until only Stages 1 and 2 of NREM plus REM sleep are returned to by the end of the night. This 90-minute cycle is the ultradian rhythm of sleep.

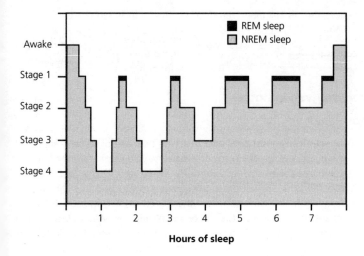

Figure 4.1 **The rhythmic pattern of stages within a night's sleep**

Note: By the end of the night only Stages 1–2 and REM sleep are
occurring.

Whether we wake up remembering what we were dreaming of may
depend on whether we awaken from our last bout of REM sleep –
remembering the dream – or from NREM sleep.

Other terms for REM sleep

Dement and Kleitman observed that REM sleep is associated with a
highly active brain while at the same time the body's muscles are effectively paralysed so there is virtually no movement. They coined the
term **paradoxical sleep** to describe this apparent contradiction. The
paradox is that at a time when the brain is full of activity the body is
not. Some modern researchers would prefer that REM sleep, being so
different from the other stages, was called Stage 5 sleep.

Meddis (1979) used a different labelling. He called NREM sleep
quiet sleep and REM sleep **active sleep**. These terms refer to the brain
activity as shown by the EEG traces. He further subdivided quiet

sleep into light quiet sleep (LQS) with synchronised slow patterns of EEG traces and deep quiet sleep (DQS) with larger, regular wave-like EEG traces. Stage 2 sleep would be LQS and Stage 4 would be DQS, and AS (active sleep) would include both Stage 1 and REM sleep.

Sleep-deprivation studies

Non-human animals

Jouvet (1967) used cats and other animals in his experiments. He arranged flowerpots, upside down, in a large tank of water with only a small amount of the pots above the water level. When cats were put into the tank they swam quickly and got out of the water, sitting upright on the exposed pots, showing their well-known dislike of getting wet. However, they were left on the pots and eventually fell asleep. At first they were all right, seemingly dozing and presumably in NREM sleep with muscles which could still just about support the body. But as they went into REM sleep and their muscles became slack – the effective paralysis mentioned earlier – their bodies slumped and they slid into the water. This of course woke them and they climbed out again. This cycle was repeated and quite soon the cats learned to awaken as soon as their heads began to nod.

The cats who kept themselves from going into normal REM sleep started to show abnormal behaviour, such as high levels of stress, and eventually they died. Jouvet was looking for evidence of the need for sleep, and this and similar studies were interpreted as demonstrating the essential nature of sleep, namely that REM sleep is essential for life and without it life becomes impossible.

Evaluation

Nowadays many of us find ethical concerns in this sort of research, and the validity of the research has also been questioned. It has been argued that this and similar experiments had such low **ecological validity** that it is not possible to draw any conclusion relating to life outside the laboratory. Also, given the well-documented strong aversion cats have to getting wet, and also the fact that they were trapped in the tank, it is highly likely that they suffered from high levels of stress from the environment as well as the lack of REM sleep. This

stress alone could well have produced the abnormal behaviour and even the deaths – it certainly would have contributed. Selye's (1956) General Adaptation Syndrome (GAS) proposed that prolonged stress leads to a state of physiological and psychological collapse.

Rats also soon die if they are deprived of sleep. They suffer physiologically, showing a breakdown of the normal control of, for example, body temperature (Hobson, 1995). Another study where rats were selectively deprived either of all sleep or of just REM sleep showed that this led to a combination of increased food intake but also weight loss, as well as the breakdown of temperature control, leading to death after four weeks (Rechtschaffen *et al.*, 1989). But still it is not possible to say that all these ill effects were the results only of sleep deprivation and that other factors such as stress were not involved.

Human participants

An early experiment was Dement's (1960) study of eight volunteers who were monitored at night and woken every time they went into REM sleep. The first night this involved being woken an average of twelve times, but by the seventh night this went up to twenty-six times, more than double. This was seen as an indication of the vital nature of REM sleep, the need for REM sleep growing stronger the more the participants were deprived of it.

Dement reported that participants exhibited only minor and temporary behaviour changes associated with this loss of REM sleep. Though interestingly, he initially reported some significant disturbances in behaviour. Later he realised that these symptoms had been, as it were, wishful thinking – what is known as the effects of experimenter expectations – and corrected himself. He had expected that sleep deprivation would result in disturbed behaviour and these expectations apparently led him to make biased observations.

Evaluation

The very final consequences of sleep deprivation in non-human animals are not necessarily shown in humans, but then human research participants are treated differently. Many studies have been done involving depriving human participants of some or all sleep and, though a temporary degree of dysfunction has sometimes

43

resulted, this has not been life-threatening or, of course, the study would have been stopped at an early stage. Researchers would not want harm to come to their participants as this would not be morally right, and also would reflect badly on them and their research. In recent years participants have been protected from psychological or physical harm by guidelines set out by the relevant authorities. In Britain these are issued by the British Psychological Association (1990) and are binding on all psychological research in Britain since 1990. The BPS has also issued similar guidelines controlling the use of non-human animals.

Case studies

Three case studies of severe sleep deprivation are well known and demonstrate various effects of going without sleep for prolonged periods.

Gulevich *et al.* (1966) reported a 17-year-old young man, Randy Gardner, who was able to stay awake for 264 hours (11 days!). This seems to be the record for sleep deprivation! As the days went by Gardner developed blurred speech and vision – a combination of perceptual and cognitive faults. He mistook some objects for people and showed what have been described as symptoms of mild paranoia, such as feeling people were labelling him as stupid because of his cognitive difficulties. But he did not have a complete mental breakdown and recovered swiftly after a good sleep. He did not catch up on all the sleep he had lost, sleeping for only 15 hours the first night and in total making up just a quarter of the lost sleep. Most of this was in Stage 4 NREM and in REM sleep – two thirds of the former and half the latter. This does indicate that these are the types of sleep which are most necessary, which have important functions, but does not of course tell us what those functions are; though maybe Stages 1–3 NREM sleep are needed as the pathway into Stage 4 and REM sleep.

Peter Tripp was another case study, reported by Dement (1972). Tripp was a DJ who stayed awake for 200 hours as a publicity stunt in New York's Times Square. Dement observed quite severe paranoid psychosis developing, with Tripp having delusions such as of being poisoned. Tripp also rushed out of the building and tried to throw himself under traffic. His personality seemed to alter after his sleep-deprivation stunt, compared to how he was before it. This is very different from Gardner's experience and could, for instance, be an illustration of individual differences, or of expectation as Tripp might have expected to experience strange sensations and so on, whereas Gardner might not.

In the third and very different case study Lugaresi *et al.* (1986) followed the progression of sleep deprivation in a man who became unable to sleep at the age of 52. This was a sudden onset and the sufferer became more and more exhausted, and finally developed a fatal lung infection. After death a post-mortem was done and lesions were found in two areas of the thalamus (forebrain) linked to sleep and hormonally controlled circadian rhythms. The neurones in these areas were fairly comprehensively destroyed. This case could be interpreted simplistically as death due to sleep deprivation alone. However it is more likely that, though the sleep deprivation had major effects including increasing stress which in turn increases susceptibility to infection, the neurones which died could have had further-reaching influence than affecting only sleep circuits. Some of these neurones quite probably were linked to other behaviours, some could have been part of other neural pathways. Some of these behaviours and pathways could also have been necessary for life. This is purely speculation but warns us that we should not assume that the lack of sleep *caused* death – it is possible that there were other associated factors.

Evaluation

The above are extreme cases where sleep was suddenly stopped and, as with any case study, one cannot really generalise to the normal population from isolated cases, even though there are now several cases of individuals staying awake for many days without long-term adverse effects.

Experimental studies

Experimental studies have taken a less totalitarian route and have looked at a gradual deprivation of sleep – from which there seem to have been few if any major negative effects. Webb and Bonnet's (1978) studies started with participants being deprived of just 2 hours sleep, after which they reported feeling fine, though they did fall asleep more quickly the next night and then slept for longer. Participants were also put on a two-month programme of gradual sleep reduction, from an initial 8 hours a night sleep down to a final 4 hours. They reported no adverse effects, which does seem to indicate that we have a remarkable ability to do without sleep if we have to.

On the other hand, self-reporting is not a method for collecting reliable data. It is not possible to be sure of its objectivity – in fact, as Popper (1969) says, it is likely that humans cannot be truly objective. Also, there could well have been demand characteristics: the participants could have felt an expectation from the researchers for certain findings. It might also have been the case that some participants might have responded in a 'macho' way – they might have felt that to admit to adverse effects would be seen as being wimpish.

Conclusion

Overall the research seems to show that we do need to sleep, regularly, in order to feel and behave in our normal way. The actual amount of sleep per night averages out at about 7–8 hours in total, but there is considerable variation between individuals. Expectation seems to be a powerful factor here, as in other of our behaviours, and if we expect to be able to cope with less sleep than usual then we are likely to find this happens. When making up lost sleep we do not show a need to catch up on all the sleep lost, but only on some of it. This is known as the **REM-rebound effect** as most of the caught-up sleep is REM sleep plus the Stage 4 NREM sleep leading into REM.

Huber-Weidman (1976) produced an overview of the findings of a large number of sleep-deprivation studies, summarised in Table 4.1. It is important to realise that the symptoms of these deprivations are more psychological than physiological for people who have been deprived of sleep for just a few days. It is also important to recognise that many if not most of the effects are due to REM deprivation alone rather than total sleep deprivation.

Core sleep

Horne (1988) proposed a model which is a bridge between a theory of sleep and sleep-deprivation studies. He suggested that most of us have more sleep than we need. It has been proposed that people sleep because their bodies need time to replenish biochemicals which have

Table 4.1 Overview of sleep-deprivation studies	
Nights without sleep	Effects
1	People do not feel comfortable, but can tolerate one night's sleep-loss.
2	People feel a much greater urge to sleep, especially when the body-temperature rhythm is lowest at 3–5 a.m.
3	Cognitive tasks are much more difficult, especially giving attention to boring ones. This is worst in the very early hours.
4	**Micro-sleep** periods start to occur, lasting about 3 seconds, during which the person stares blankly into space and temporarily loses awareness. They become irritable and confused.
5	As well as what is described above, the person may start to experience delusions, though cognitive ability (for example, problem-solving) is all right.
6	The person starts to lose their sense of identity, be depersonalised. This is known as sleep-deprivation psychosis.
Source: After Huber-Wiedman (1976).	

been used during the day, the **restoration theory** of sleep (described in Chapter 5). Horne pointed out that in fact cell restoration takes place during the day as well as at night, so it might be that only *some* of our sleep is necessary, perhaps the early hours of sleep. Horne called this **core sleep**. He bases this on an older study where groups of participants were allowed 6 weeks on a fixed amount of sleep per night. One group slept for 4 hours nightly, a second group for 6 hours and the third group for 7.5 hours. Participants did a variety of cognitive tests before and after the experimental sleep period, and only the 4-hour people showed any effect at the end, a minor drop in memory. Horne concluded that we need only about 5-hours sleep a night; the rest is what he termed optional and could be omitted without ill effects.

If one looks back to page 41 to see the pattern of sleep stages through the night, it seems that Horne is suggesting that our Stage 4 NREM sleep is vital, but only about half of our REM sleep is needed. This is a novel idea and could link in with the minor consequences of short-term sleep deprivation, but does not fit in with most other data showing the REM-rebound effect. Also, long-term loss of REM sleep is associated with psychological dysfunction such as hallucinations or waking dreams, which also does not support Horne's proposal.

A last thought

Recent research has suggested an extra and different effect, that too much sleep can impair our performance and even lead to or be part of psychological disorders. Increased REM sleep is a feature of many people with **unipolar depression** and the drugs called tricyclic antide-pressants which successfully lift this disorder selectively block and therefore reduce REM sleep, without interfering with NREM sleep. Pinel (1993) cites this as evidence that REM sleep deprivation is not harmful. Alternatively it could be that the increased REM sleep before treatment was part of the problem, that is it was in some way part of the depression, and the tricyclics are beneficial by their action of reducing this extra REM sleep.

Summary

Sleep is not one phenomenon but several. It can be divided into REM (rapid eye movement) sleep, when we dream the most, and NREM sleep when the eyes are fairly still and we do not seem to dream much. NREM sleep has four stages, each with its own characteristic electro-encephalogram (EEG) pattern. Stage 1 is when we start to fall asleep; Stages 2 and 3 are deeper stages of sleep, and Stage 4 is the deepest. REM sleep does not have stages. It has a fast EEG trace as the brain becomes very active, but the body is effectively paralysed and is quiet.

Research has shown that deprivation is associated with detri-mental effects, varying from minor, short-term perceptual problems to major and lasting personality changes. However, it is not clear how much of these are specifically caused by total sleep deprivation, by REM deprivation or by other causes such as expectation. The methodology and extremely unusual conditions of many studies make it difficult to gain generalisable conclusions.

Horne has suggested a different concept of core and optional sleep which is interesting and ties in with some findings but not with others.

1 Copy out and complete the following table:

Type of sleep	NREM 1	NREM 2	NREM 3	NREM 4	REM
Duration in minutes					
Brain-wave pattern					
Heart- and breathing-rate					
Can the body move?					
Meddis' terminology					

2 How long does each cycle of NREM and REM sleep last? What other cycle could this tie in with (see Chapter 2)?

Further reading

Gribbin, M. (1990) All in a night's sleep. *New Scientist: Inside Science* 36, 7 July, http://www.newscientist.com/ (Has a good, illustrated overview of knowledge and research into sleep.)

bisleep.medsch.ucla.edu/ (A variety of interesting links to sleep topics.)

5

Theories of sleep

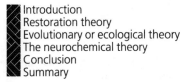
Introduction

The previous chapter explains some of what goes on when we sleep and what can happen if we do not have enough sleep, but we also need to consider explanations of why we sleep. In addition we should consider ideas on why it is that the amount of sleep we have varies not only with age but also individually from one person to another.

Three main theories of sleep are current. They are the restoration theory, the **evolutionary theory** (or ecological theory) and the **neuro-chemical theory**, though this latter is more a model of the physiological control of sleep (*how* we sleep) than a strict theory which explains *why* we sleep.

Restoration theory

Most of us would agree that after a physically or mentally strenuous day we are much more ready to go to sleep and may well sleep longer than usual. Oswald (1970, 1976) suggested that both REM and NREM sleep serve the purpose of restoring and replenishing our bodies and brains. In other words, we sleep to restore ourselves physiologically and psychologically. He suggests that NREM sleep is needed more for restoring bodily processes which have deteriorated or been worn down by the day and REM sleep is the main time for renewing brain processes and replenishing neurochemicals used up in the day that need to be regenerated by protein synthesis.

Support for the theory

This sounds both logical and sensible, and is supported by empirical evidence. Babies and fetuses sleep with both REM and NREM rhythms for a far greater proportion of their day than older children or adults, and it is in these very early stages that both bodies and neural connections are growing fastest. Not only do young babies spend on average about 18 hours a day sleeping, as opposed to about 8 hours in adults, but also they spend about half of those 18 hours in REM sleep whereas adults spend about a quarter of sleep in REM. This ties in with the larger amount of activity in the developing brain with much protein synthesis needed for cell and synaptic growth. Also, both physical repair and brain-protein synthesis are dependent on **growth hormone** which is secreted after the first burst of delta activity in slow-wave sleep (Oswald, 1980). This is interesting support for the old wives' tale that we grow in our sleep!

Further support of the restoration theory comes from knowledge that patients who have had physiological assaults on their brains from drug overdoses or from electroconvulsive therapy then spend an increased time in REM sleep, perhaps to synthesise the brain-proteins (for example, neurotransmitters) which have been lost or damaged, or are needed for repair. And bloodflow to the brain does increase in REM sleep which could be to bring in extra oxygen, glucose and nutrients for the suggested protein synthesis.

In addition there is evidence from studies of learning that REM sleep is related to learning and the consolidation of memory. For example, Bloch (1976) showed that rats who were given complex maze-tasks daily had increased REM sleep. Learning is related to protein synthesis.

Problems with the theory

On the other hand, it is known that amino acids (the building blocks for proteins and many neurochemicals) are not stored by the body and only last in the body for about 4 hours after a meal. This means that protein synthesis might be halted by halfway through the night's sleep because the amino acids run out.

If restoration was the only function of sleep then we would expect to find consistent effects from sleep deprivation. However, as we saw in the last chapter, this is not the case. People certainly don't need to make up the sleep they have lost, though they do appear to need the REM sleep or core sleep most particularly (the REM-rebound effect). It may also be that some recovery and manufacture of biochemicals takes place during the day when one is relaxed and quiet. It has been suggested that people often experience bursts of micro-sleep during the day.

If restoration was the only function of sleep we would also expect to find that the more active you were during the day the more you slept at night. Research suggests that there is no relationship. For example, Shapiro *et al.* (1981) recorded the sleep duration of marathon runners. After a race they showed decreases in REM sleep but did show more slow-wave sleep. Horne and Minard (1985) engaged participants in numerous physical activities but found no increases in sleep, though the participants went to sleep faster. It may be that slow-wave sleep is important for recovery after vigorous activity (Carlson, 1986).

The sleep patterns of some animals raise further questions for restoration theory. If sleep serves a universal purpose, why are there so many variations in the way that animals sleep? For example, dolphins have evolved unique sleep patterns to overcome the real risk of drowning. Those in the river Indus take naps of a few seconds at a time, repeatedly, throughout the 24 hours of a day. This is probably also related to their need for vigilance at all times as so much large debris is always sweeping down the river (Pilleri, 1979) and if this hit them they could be seriously injured. A 1984 study showed that marine dolphins sleep with only one hemisphere at a time, so half the cortex is always awake, presumably to organise surfacing to breathe (Mukhametov, 1984). This is a valuable, in fact essential adaptation in an air-breathing but aquatic animal. Empson (1993) reported similar findings for porpoises.

Empson has the view that, in spite of all this, the overall evidence supports sleep-as-synthesis, even though there are suggestions that the high levels of brain activity in REM sleep are likely to consume all the glucose and oxygen available, leaving no margin for growth or repair.

An alternative restoration theory

Professor David Maurice of Columbia University, New York, has another idea (Maurice, 1998). He suggested that REM sleep happens because otherwise during sleep the fluid inside the eyes would not circulate and the eyes might become internally short of the oxygen borne by this fluid. Moving the eyeballs sets up tiny currents in this fluid and ensures the delivery of oxygen to the cornea. This would explain why fetuses have REM sleep, and why periods of REM sleep become slightly longer in adults as the night progresses. But it doesn't explain why experimental participants deprived of REM sleep then have no eye problems reported and also have an increased amount of REM sleep when allowed to sleep naturally. Nor does it explain why participants deprived of both types of sleep 'catch up' on more REM than NREM sleep (see Chapter 4).

Evolutionary or ecological theory

The evolutionary or ecological theory, suggested by Meddis (1975, 1979), proposes that sleep could be a time of increased safety as animals are immobile and therefore less likely to be noticed by predators. We are all aware of how difficult it is to keep still for any length of time and movement, it is suggested, could attract unwelcome notice. So Meddis suggests that to be more or less still when it is too dark to see either food or threats could be an advantage for some animals.

However some animals do not appear, at first, to fit with this theory. What about those animals who sleep in the day and are nocturnal in habit? Some of them, such as owls, are specialised to see well in low light, or there are others who, like bats, are not dependent on light to find food or to be aware of their environment. These animals have evolved sleep patterns which fit in with their way of life, that is they sleep during the day in places of safety such as caves or burrows. So their sleep patterns still fit in with an evolutionary theory.

Also, there are those who have no predators to fear, such as lions (Lloyd *et al.*, 1984). Lions appear relatively happy to sleep wherever and whenever they can.

Grazing animals also appear not to fit in with the theory because they sleep very little. Animals such as cows and antelopes spend most of their time grazing in herds. Perhaps for these animals remaining still in such large numbers on a wide open field or plain would present too much of a sitting target. So not remaining vigilant could be seriously maladaptive. Therefore, as they are constantly at serious risk from predators, this lack of sleep would also seem to back Meddis' theory concerning safety. On the other hand, we also know that the nutritional value of vegetation is very poor and in order to survive these grazers have to keep eating for most of each 24-hour period. If they did not – if they stopped to sleep – they would be lacking in nutrition and energy the next day.

Evaluation

How does this relate to humans? The idea is that when we lived truly wild, when our distant ancestors were evolving, those who were able to sleep at night survived better as they were less likely to become prey for carnivores. They had conserved their energies when it was too dark to see and had been successfully hidden from predators. These survivors passed on to their descendants the ability to sleep through the night and therefore survive. Maybe the adage could be rewritten as those who sleep the night away live to feed another day!

So this theory suggests that sleep is an evolutionary leftover. On the other hand, if being very still and unnoticeable was the great benefit and survival tactic of sleep then it is puzzling that so many humans sleep noisily. In fact, a whole industry has sprung up based on reducing or curing snoring! The main theory also fails to explain why after sleep deprivation we sleep for longer, maybe even falling asleep in daylight, as it would suggest that we would not need to catch up on missed sleep if there was adequate light.

If protection was the only function of sleep we would expect to find that animals who are likely to be attacked sleep rather little. In general predators do sleep more than those who are preyed upon, but taken to the extreme the principle suggests that some animals shouldn't sleep at all in order to be safe.

As we saw in Chapter 4, Horne (1988) has suggested a variation by saying that there could be two types of sleep: core or essential sleep and optional sleep. Each of them would have different adaptive functions. But this theory as a whole is still basically conjecture and it is difficult to see how empirical evidence could be obtained.

Meddis also suggests that the much longer sleep-patterns of babies evolved to prevent exhaustion in their mothers. This certainly sounds nice, but it does not explain the survival of the non-sleepy trait in babies, nor the variation in quantities and type of sleep in people of all ages.

Empson (1989) described Meddis' theory as a 'waste of time' theory, meaning that the theory suggested sleep was a waste of time (he may even have meant that the theory was a waste of time!). Empson pointed out that sleep is universal among animals, even the most successful predators, and that sleep deprivation can on occasion be fatal. This suggests that sleep has some value. On the other hand, we could ask whether it is really such an advantage, when avoiding predation, to be effectively paralysed and senseless for hours. One can see the advantage of staying still and quiet in the dark, and thus avoiding danger. But to be almost unconscious, unaware of one's surroundings, could be interpreted as being more, not less, vulnerable. Certainly stories from India of man-eating lions preying on sleeping rather than waking victims does not fit in with this theory.

Horne also suggests that sleep may perform different functions in different species or different sizes of animal, such as in aquatic animals, grazing animals and those with higher intellects. If this is so, then to look for a global explanation of sleep is rather pointless. On the other hand, the fact that animals such as dolphins appear to develop sleep-adaptations specific to their environments suggests that there are evolutionary principles at work. Sleep must be serving a purpose and each species evolves a means of sleeping in such a way that doesn't also threaten their survival.

The neurochemical theory

The neurochemical approach or theory suggests that sleep has a particular function(s) within the brain, a specialised sort of restoration theory.

REM sleep

This seems to be related to a noradrenaline pathway going up through the brain. We know that a feature of depression is that sufferers have unusually large amounts of REM sleep. It has also been found that REM deprivation can relieve depression (Vogel, 1975). This suggests some link between too much REM and depression. Some drugs which are used successfully to treat depression – like the tricyclic antidepressants – have been also been found to reduce REM sleep. Triclyics stimulate noradrenergic pathways and therefore the production of noradrenaline. What the drugs may be doing is performing the functions of REM sleep and therefore less REM sleep is needed and, for whatever reason, the reduced REM sleep alleviates depression. Parallel studies in non-human animals show that reducing noradrenaline in the brain increases REM sleep. In other words, there is an association between REM and noradrenaline – REM sleep has a neurological purpose, to replenish the brain's noradrenaline levels which were depleted by the day's activities.

NREM sleep

The brain neurotransmitter serotonin has been shown to be linked with NREM or slow-wave sleep. If serotonin is removed using drugs, the amount of NREM sleep is also reduced. So we could conclude that a serotonin-dependent pathway controls NREM sleep and that we need serotonin in order to have NREM sleep. This is also backed up by evidence from depressive patients. A typical feature of unipolar depression is the inability to fall asleep – staying tired but awake every night well into the small hours – and sleep when it finally comes lasting for only a short time. Some of the modern drugs which successfully treat depression, the SSRIs (selective serotonin reuptake inhibitors) such as Prozac, increase the activity of serotonin in the brain and restore both the sleep patterns and the person's mood.

Evaluation

But what is the purpose of all this? Experiments by Greene at Harvard suggest that sleep is linked to tiny molecules, appearing within all cells including neurones, which are the source of energy for the cell to work – sort of molecular torch-batteries (Holmes, 1997). These molecules are called ATP, made of **adenosine** with three phosphate (hence triphosphate) molecules attached to it. Adenosine could be the key to 'why' we sleep, as in cats at any rate when adenosine levels rise above some critical level they get sleepy and sleep longer in both REM and NREM sleep. Also, during sleep levels of adenosine fall, to rise again during the waking hours.

So – putting all this together – it might be that we have NREM sleep in order to be able to go into REM sleep, and we need REM sleep to deal with adenosine to provide the brain with energy for the next day. It might be that sleep is all about homeostasis – about balancing the levels of various neurochemicals in our cells.

Conclusion

Whichever parts of whichever theories of sleep turn out in the end to be true there is no denying the necessity of sleep. Hobson (1995) suggested a way to put together what is known. He proposed a three-tier analysis of sleep.

1   At the behavioural level, sleep conserves energy when foraging for food or finding a mate are likely to be difficult, or when ambient temperatures fall. In other words, sleep is useful when conditions become less favourable to the animal. It is also a time when pair-bonded or family groups can reinforce the relationship by being together, during the period leading up to sleep as well as when actually asleep.
2   Hobson suggested a developmental level where brain structures and connections can grow and mature before they are needed in action. This clearly ties in with restoration ideas.
3   At the metabolic level there are various physiological changes such as alterations in blood pressure and release of hormones involved in sleep.

Whether this different way of studying sleep is useful only time will tell.

Summary

There are three main theories of sleep – sleep as restoration, sleep as an evolutionary behaviour and, though this is an extension of restoration, the neurochemical model for sleep.

Restoration theory was suggested by Oswald. He suggested that both REM and NREM sleep restore and/or replenish our brains and bodies. Neurochemicals are resynthesised during sleep and growth hormone secreted. There is evidence supporting this theory, but also some which does not, such as studies which fail to link sleep with amounts of activity the day before. Non-human animal studies also show mixed support for this theory.

Meddis' ecological or evolutionary theory suggests sleep is a time of inaction so that prey can be safe from predators. Evolutionary arguments can also be applied to why babies sleep – to prevent exhaustion in their parents. However, there are many observations which simply do not fit in, though Horne overcame them to some extent by hypothesising that sleep performs different functions in different species.

The neurochemical model suggests that sleep has a specialised restoration function within the brain. REM sleep is associated with a noradrenaline pathway and evidence suggests that REM sleep might replenish noradrenaline levels in the brain. NREM sleep is associated with serotonin levels and might require a critical level of serotonin to be switched on.

Hobson proposed a three-tier analysis of sleep which ties together what is known about sleep, giving sleep behavioural, developmental and metabolic levels of function.

Review exercise

For each theory make a heading, then add a list of bullet points to include:

1 The main researcher proposing the theory.
2 A one-sentence outline of the theory.
3 Points supporting the theory.
4 Points against the theory.

Further reading

Gregory, R. and Zangwill, O.L. (1987) *The Oxford Companion to the Mind*. London: Oxford University Press. (This has many useful sections on various theories and other topics to do with sleep.)

Theories of dreaming

Introduction

Dreams are fascinating. For many thousands of years humans have been intrigued by the bizarre world which we enter through sleep, and all sorts of explanations have been and are suggested for this biorhythmic behaviour. We dream mostly, but not exclusively, in REM sleep, and we know that in this state the brain is buzzing with activity but the body is effectively paralysed. Dreams and dreaming are a fascinating area of psychology which is full of contradictory hypotheses and interesting questions: what are dreams? Are they purposeful neurophysiological processes or random firings of brain activity? Do dreams and/or REM sleep serve a special purpose, such as consolidation of memory or processing of the day's information? Does the content of dreams have special meaning?

One point to be clear about in the following theories is whether they are referring to dreams or REM sleep, or both.

Neurobiological theories

Hobson and McCarley's (1977) activation–synthesis theory

Rose's (1976) neural theory suggested that dreams are just the result of the brain's random firing of neurones. These firings then trigger memories and the brain makes a sequence or narrative out of this mixture. This idea was expressed in more detail by Hobson and McCarley (1977) in their two-part **activation–synthesis theory**. Hobson and McCarley suggested that during REM sleep the neurones in the brain are spontaneously active (as always) – a sort of 'neural noise'. This is the activation part of their theory. However, in the absence of associated external stimuli, the brain then tries to make sense of this neural activity and the result of this making sense is what we call dreams. This is the synthesis. External stimuli, such as an external noise, may be incorporated into the dream along with internal stimuli, such as memories.

Evaluation

Dement and Wolpert's (1958) research supports part of this model. They showed that we are aware of some external stimuli when asleep. They sprayed water lightly on to participants in REM sleep and then, after a short interval, woke them up. The majority of them had incorporated the water into their dreams, such as dreaming they were having a walk in the rain.

It is also suggested that physiological input is incorporated as well. For example, we often represent the sensation of being paralysed (as we are in REM sleep) into our dreams as being unable to escape or run from something, or that we are falling helplessly.

A main criticism of the activation–synthesis model is that there seems no reason why NREM sleep should not include random firing of neurones and therefore also lead to dreams. We do dream during NREM sleep, but studies show this is far less frequent than during REM sleep.

Oswald's (1980) restoration model

Another neurobiological theory of REM sleep is Oswald's restoration model, which suggests that in this dreaming sleep we replenish the brain's supplies of neurochemicals, neurotransmitters and neuromodulators, used up by the previous day's activities. These need to be regenerated to provide for the next day's needs, as we saw in Chapter 5. Research studies on REM sleep link the large amount of REM sleep in fetuses and babies to the high growth-rate of their neural connections. It does seem more likely that this is what is happening to them rather than that they might be dreaming – though that could be just our own failure to be able to imagine what they might be dreaming about!

Of course, this theory only suggests what might be going on neurally whilst we dream. It does not address the question of why we have that dreaming experience, but it does explain why fetuses and babies have so much REM sleep and also explains why people have more REM sleep after mental exertion.

Crick and Mitchison's (1983) model

A further neurobiological theory was suggested by the Nobel prize-winner Francis Crick and his colleague Graeme Mitchison. Crick and Mitchison (1983) suggested that dreaming is simply the rubbish-disposal system of the brain – we dream what we discard, as we discard it. This 'garbage' consists of unwanted, that is irrelevant, or even harmful neural patterns and connections. Evans (1984) supported the Crick and Mitchison model by emphasising similarities with computer systems: the process is similar to updating memory files, deleting unwanted data or files, checking connections and so on (see below).

Crick and Mitchison went even further and hypothesised that if some of these neural connections are harmful then it would be most *inadvisable* to try and recall them – remembering your dreams could put you at risk, maybe! This idea is in direct conflict with the psychodynamic approach: as we shall see, Freud and his followers suggested that we dream in order to work through our problems.

Learning involves the laying down of new brain connections, new circuits, and not only are some likely to become irrelevant as time goes by, but also our brains are likely to make some mistakes in forming connections. So dreaming could be the brain's own self-correction therapy where the brainstem sends blasts of impulses upwards to the cortex which 'search and destroy' unwanted or inaccurate synapses. (In fact it isn't the synapses which are destroyed but rather the information pathways within them.) Our dreams are the interpretations of this, the cortex's attempts to make some narrative sense of the many and various and largely unconnected bits of information being accessed by this process. If we couldn't do this discarding, Crick and Mitchison suggest, our brains would have to be vast in size to accommodate all the extra circuitry.

Evaluation

In support of this is evidence that dolphins, who have not been shown to have REM sleep, do have unexpectedly large cerebral cortexes which could in theory house all this extra storage. In other words, they don't have REM sleep because they don't need to discard things. However, one might still wonder if they form faulty neural connections which need to be unformed.

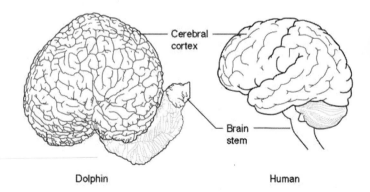

Figure 6.1 **Contrast between the relative sizes of the dolphin and human cortex**

This theory addresses the question of why we have the dreaming behaviour but does not explain why fetuses and babies have REM sleep. The theory also does not explain dreams such as the common dream of falling, why we have bizarre dreams that contain 'novel' experiences and why those who do remember their dreams seem no more dysfunctional than those who don't. Finally, the computer analogy does not really fit with modern **connectionist** ideas. There are plenty of potential connectionist pathways to accommodate vast amounts of wastage, far more than we could probably create in a lifetime. Hence there is no need to save space by discarding unwanted connections. Then again, it could just be a matter of good housekeeping.

On balance, this theory, though attractive, has little empirical evidence in its favour.

Ornstein's (1986) reorganisation of mental structures

This reorganisation of mental structures theory suggests that when we are dreaming the brain is actually consolidating the day's input, the day's learning. This input is being assimilated and the pre-existing mental structures may be modified to accommodate the new information, particularly into memory. In other words, dreaming is an effect of activity in the brain, such as synapses being altered or new synapses being made. This activity may involve the construction of new schema and this might then explain the large amounts of REM sleep in infants, who we assume to be busy making sense of their new world. It does not, however, give clues to the large amounts of REM sleep recorded in fetuses who are not likely to be formatting schema, though they are already making sense of internal and external sensations. And the typical infant rhythm of less than an hour awake followed by about three hours asleep seems to give a very generous amount of REM time (one and a half hours at 50 per cent of the total) for the short time when input is happening – unless of course infant REM sleep has additional or alternative functions to adult REM sleep. For example, it could be that the fetal brain is testing out its new synapses, new connections made as a result of the sensory input in its hour awake. So REM sleep in fetuses might be the equivalent of a road-test of circuitry before the fetus is turned out from the production line (so to speak).

Conclusion

So far we have looked at four different neurobiological theories of dreaming. Neurobiological here refers to these theories explaining our dreaming in terms of what is going on in the brain: what is happening in the neurones, in the synapses, in the transmitter and other chemicals of the nervous system. One theory links REM sleep to the resynthesis of neurochemicals; one to the removal of irrelevant or faulty connections between neurones; one to bursts of random firing of neurones; and one to the assimilation and accommodation of the day's sensory input.

Progress exercise

1 Can you sort out which description in the sentence above refers to which theory or model?
2 Two out of the four theories explain dreams as the brain's efforts at making some sort of sense out of the firing of neurones during REM sleep. Which two are they?

Psychodynamic theory

This theory is based on Freud's thoughts and views, the most important one here being that our dreams themselves have real meaning. His book, *Interpretation of Dreams* (1900), suggested that our dreams are the best way – the 'royal road' – into our powerful but hidden unconscious – the seething mass of the mind which has a controlling but secret influence on our thoughts and behaviour. He called the narrative description of a dream its **manifest content** and the true wish-fulfilment meaning its **latent content**. For example, if you dreamed of turning into a hippopotamus this is the manifest content. The latent content would be a therapist's attempt to suggest what unconscious meanings were represented. Perhaps you fear becoming very fat!

Freud hypothesised that in our dreams we realise those ideas, wishes and needs which we have buried or repressed from our conscious minds as they are in some way unacceptable to us. Maybe they are socially unacceptable, or would for some other reason fill us with guilt or anxiety. Examples of this could be the inner conflicts between our id (primitive self), ego (socialised self) and super-ego (idealised self), or those between our libido (biological desires) and thanatos (turning away from pleasure), or others such as penis envy in females or Oedipal sexual desires for the opposite-sex parent. Dreams represent these thoughts and desires and their fulfilment in a form which does not threaten us or cause us pain (Freud, 1933).

Jung's contribution

Jung, a follower of Freud who later diverged to form his own psycho-dynamic theories, suggested that in our dreams we are able to access the stored memories of all humanity, dating back to our primeval ancestry. He called this the collective unconscious. This could perhaps explain the dreams of inescapable pursuit or of falling as memories of highly emotionally charged events from other people in other times. Jung also believed that a main motivator or driving-force was not sex but the search for the spiritual and mystic. Maybe this combination of thoughts from the collective unconscious with desires for the awesome and wondrous could explain the apparently illogical narratives of dreams.

Evaluation

These ideas are clearly attractive to many as the thriving industry of dream interpretation shows. However, accounts of dreams are not verifiable, interpretations are highly subjective and this whole theory is non-testable and therefore neither provable nor refutable. Also, Freud himself viewed most latent content as centred on sexual energies. He was writing in the sexually repressed Victorian Age and it is possible that this could have been true then. But even if one accepts this, it is not possible to claim that exactly the same would be true in today's sexually more liberated climate. Hayes (1994: 265) suggested that if a society were repressed in a different way (such as regarding eating as sinful and, for instance, then ate only in private), according to psychodynamic theory, dreams should have a strong food and eating content, camouflaged to preserve mental decency!

Schatzman (1992) has another comment. He pointed out that

Freud offered different therapeutic analyses of the same dream accounts at different times. This sort of inconsistency makes it difficult to evaluate Freud's work.

Cognitive theory

Evans (1984) suggested a cognitive, information-processing approach to dreaming. The suggestion is that we are born with a brain which is pre-programmed to a limited extent. Thereafter each individual has a set of personal experiences which produce corresponding changes in our neural networks. So when we sleep and there is a respite from the vast sensory input of the waking state, there is a window of opportunity for the brain to catch up on its 'filing' systems. In this there is a close parallel with Ornstein's theory, described above. Evans suggested that sleep (and REM sleep in particular) is when the brain can be more or less off-line, and in this state programs can be run, updated, re-indexed and cross-referenced. Our dreams are the effects of periodic reconnection – the brain coming on-line for a brief spell so that small portions of the programs which are running can be sampled. Our brain then fits them into a narrative account as best it can, and this is what we experience as dreams. We do this because it is a feature of our cognitive processes generally. For example, sensory data are generally received in an incomplete state and our mind has the task of making sense of them on the basis of past experience. The same would be true of how we deal with nonsensical and incomplete dream material, and this explanation could just as well apply to Ornstein's theory.

Evaluation

One example cited as support for Evans' model is that of problem-solving in our sleep. 'Sleep on it' is common advice to someone with a problem, and one man who reported the success of this was the organic chemist Kekule. No one had been able to work out just how carbon atoms could join together to form all the many complex organic molecules, even basic ones like benzene. Kekule fell asleep puzzling over this and dreamt of a ring of snakes, linked each with the tail of the one in front in its own mouth. When he awoke he remembered the dream and made the leap of thought to applying this to carbon atoms. Rings of carbon were suggested and found to be the basis of life.

Hopfield (1984) strengthened the computer analogy with actual computer simulations of learning experiments. He found that, if computers were fed additional and unnecessary data for a task but allowed some sort of discarding before the task was done, they processed the necessary information more efficiently than if the discarding was not first done. One criticism of this evidence is that comparisons between the highly complex human brain and relatively simplistic mechanistic models have limited value. But this approach is currently attracting much attention as the computer 'neural' networks become increasingly more complex and therefore more analogous to the human brain.

Lucid dreaming

Some theories of dreaming suggest that a dream is something which happens to you. In lucid dreaming it is suggested that it is a cognitive process of which you are in control. There have always been anecdotal reports of people within the dreaming state being able actively manipulate and/or take part in their dreams. This implies being conscious as well as dreaming, which seems an **oxymoron** (a figure of speech where apparently contradictory terms appear in conjunction, such as 'make haste slowly'). Once this idea of lucid dreaming (Van Eeden, 1913) was part of fringe- or para-psychology, but recently research on such dreaming has appeared in mainstream psychological journals. Van Eeden reported that in lucid dreaming 'the sleeper reaches a state of perfect awareness and is able to direct his attention … yet the sleep … is undisturbed, deep and refreshing'.

The paradox of having moving eyes and an active brain combined together with paralysed muscles seemed to preclude any investigation of this phenomenon, until Hearne (1980) tried to use the ability of the eyes to move as a signal from the sleeper to the researcher. One participant, Alan Worsley, succeeded in moving his eyes eight times in a left-and-right manner to signal that he was both lucid and dreaming. He was connected up to an EEG machine so that his periods of REM sleep were being recorded and the appearance of this eight-times pattern also showed on the EEG trace, most often early in the morning at about 6.30 a.m. after about half an hour of ordinary

REM sleep. Later research linked the lucid periods with high-arousal, presumably vivid, REM sleep. Similar research was being done in the USA but major journals refused to publish it for five years (LaBerge, 1985).

Though lucid dreaming is not a special physiological state, it does seem to be a special state and surveys show that about 50 per cent of the population have experienced at least one lucid dream in their lifetime (Blackmore, 1988). The critical factor in recognising a lucid dream is to recollect that during the dream one questioned its reality and decided, during the dream, that it was not real – it was a dream (Blackmore, 1991).

Some lucid dreams can be an extraordinary combination of lucidity and dreaming. Schatzman *et al.* (1988) reported another of Worsley's lucid dreams in which his task was to give himself a series of small electric shocks when in the lucid state. Worsley then reported becoming lucid whilst dreaming that he was sleeping outside in a sleeping-bag (he was of course actually indoors) when it started to rain. First he thought he was truly awake and therefore should not cheat and set off the shocks. Then he worried that the electric shock machine might get damaged if the rain made it wet. It was not reported if he became concerned about the machine short-circuiting, but he did set off the shocks!

Common dreams of false awakenings, where the person dreams vividly and in detail that they wake up, get up, wash, dress and so on, are said to be similar to lucid dreams in that people feel they are conscious within these dreams. And research suggests that people who have this sort of dream of false awakenings are also more likely to have out-of-body experiences (OBEs) (Blackmore, 1988). Gackenbach and LaBerge (1988) and Gackenbach (1994) suggested that lucid dreaming may also explain UFO-abduction and near-death experiences (NDEs). All these could be the result of mental lucidity occurring whilst in a dream/hallucinatory state. However, Blackmore (1996) pointed out that in a lucid dream one is aware one is dreaming, but with OBEs people can feel some confusion and with false awakenings, UFO-abductions and NDEs they feel awake.

Conclusion

Overall it is clear that dreaming is a very different state of consciousness to waking, whatever the cause or reason for dreams. In his overview of this area, Empson (1993) has pointed out four main differences between these two states:

1 We are the spectators of our dreams, we do not consciously control them. Lucid dreaming is an example of being a spectator.
2 Normal logic simply does not apply in dreams.
3 Normal dreams are rich, varied and bizarre compared to dreams monitored in a laboratory setting. This 'laboratory effect' means that much of our research-data lacks ecological validity.
4 Dreams contain hallucinations, delusions, amnesia, and exclude the awareness of lots that is going on and streams of consciousness which we have when awake.

Summary

Dreams fascinate humanity. Psychologists have proposed a variety of theories to account for why we dream.

The four neurobiological theories are:

1 Hobson and McCarley's theory that the random firing of brain neurones is given meaning by your mind (activation and synthesis).
2 Oswald's restoration model which ties dreaming in with replenishing neurochemicals in the brain.
3 Crick and Mitchison's theory that sees dreaming as a garbage-disposal effect where the brain seeks out and destroys unwanted or faulty connections, and dreams are the side-effect of this.
4 Ornstein's model likens the brain to a complex filing system which needs updating after each day. Dreams are again a side-effect.

Psychodynamic theory regards dreams as a valuable insight into our unconscious desires, guilt and anxiety, which surface concealed in fantasy. Dreams can be used by a psychoanalyst to free a person from their unconscious motives. However, it is difficult to see any way of testing this approach.

Cognitive theory is almost a further development of Ornstein's neurobiological idea. Evans uses the computer as an analogy for brain activity and regards dreaming as a time of updating files on the day's input. Programs, or brain pathways, can be tested and run, and information can be processed, re-indexed and so on. Dreams are the effects of periodic bursts of such trials and tests.

Lucid dreaming is a subset of dreaming, where the dreamer is consciously aware and in control of the dream. Research, once scorned, has become accepted and some experimental evidence is quite strong. There are links to out-of-body experiences of various kinds.

Review exercise

Match up the main theories with the appropriate key concepts.

Theories	Key concepts
Hobson and McCarley	consolidating the day's input
Oswald	assimilating and reorganising data
Crick and Mitchison	replenishing neurochemicals
Ornstein	a rubbish-disposal system
Psychodynamic	brain making sense of its random firings
Cognitive (Evans)	expression of hidden fears and desires

Make a table for each theory as follows:

Name of theory, proposer and date	Key concept	Evidence supporting	Evidence against

Further reading

Alvarez, A. (1995) *Night: An exploration of night life, night language, sleep and dreams*. London: Cape. (This is a useful book containing many ideas.)

Prentice, P. (1995) Dream analysis. *Psychology Review* 2 (1), 12–15. (This is an interesting article from the psychodynamic viewpoint.)

States, B. (1997) *Seeing in the Dark: Reflections on dreams and dreaming*. New Haven and London: Yale University Press. (A comprehensive work as well as a personal view on dreaming.)

www.sawaka.com/spiritwatch/luciddreams.htm (Has an excellent reference article by Susan Blackmore on lucid dreaming.)

7

Disrupting bodily rhythms

Introduction

This chapter will look at what happens when bodily rhythms are disturbed. How does this affect our behaviour and what have psychologists suggested we do to cope better? The material is interesting in its own right and has important applications, for example considering the effects of jet lag on airline pilots. This chapter will also provide you with evidence for discussing sleep and dream states and the theories of sleep and dreaming.

Humans are very adaptable. We have successfully colonised all but the most inhospitable regions of our world and are able to cope with extremes of temperature. We also can adapt to many and various day-length situations. Those who live in temperate zones cope with the changes from long days and short nights in summer to the opposite in winter, whereas those in equatorial regions have very little variation in day-length. And the people who inhabit the regions inside the Arctic Circle have summer weeks when the sun never sets and winter weeks of unremitting darkness. However, this latter may not be so easily adjusted to. After all, most of us cheer up and feel more positive on a sunny day and the thought of weeks of darkness is not really appealing!

In Chapter 2 we saw that we ourselves are rhythmic, as well as being sensitive to the rhythms of the world around us, such as meal-times and also dawn and dusk. So how do we adapt if there is no dawn and no dusk? There is a suggestion that some of us cope better than others, that there is individual difference in the extent to which we can adapt. For example, statistics in Finland, a country where the sun does not rise above the horizon for several weeks in winter, show that there is a very high suicide rate and also a large problem with abuse of alcohol. Is this a sign that people are finding the extreme rhythm of a night that lasts for weeks affects their minds and behaviour? This could be so, and there is a possible link with a recognised condition described below.

SAD (seasonal affective disorder)

This behavioural disorder, known as SAD, affects a number of people who experience serious depression as autumn approaches and shorter days set in, recovering only when spring brings more and stronger daylight. This is a serious clinical condition, far more than the slight lowering of mood many experience on overcast or dull days.

Case study

In a 1988 BBC documentary, Blakemore described the case of an individual with SAD, studied at the Maryland National Institute of Mental Health. Pat Moore had suffered from unipolar depression for many years before she became aware that her depression was seasonal, arriving with the start of winter and lifting when spring came. This was no minor mood-change, but a strong emotional swing so severe that her whole life was affected and her ability to function deeply impaired. In winter she would sleep for 12 hours a day and when awake she had little energy, less enthusiasm and felt her life held no pleasure.

Blakemore suggested that we humans could be sensitive to day-length in the same way as some plants are, as well as many of the animals whose behaviour changes with the seasons. Chapter 3 explains how the brain detects daylight and therefore, we can assume, day-length also. The idea that a factor as simple as daylight/day-length could be responsible for Pat's condition was then tested with her full co-operation. As autumn arrived she would wake early, using an alarm clock, get up and sit for a few hours listening to the radio. The key thing was that she listened to the radio sitting in front of a bank of full-spectrum lights which bathed her in bright white light as similar as possible to natural light. The result was astonishing. Pat reported feeling less down within just days of starting the treatment. After some weeks she was feeling herself again, having regained her energy and positive feelings even though it was still winter. She went from saying, 'I don't seem to have a good period of time ... and don't see a future right now' to 'I feel fine now, sleeping about six hours a night ... and then sit in front of the light box ... I feel something has been turned on in my brain that says ... it's time to live!' (Blakemore, 1988b).

Evaluation

This suggests that not only is the brain very sensitive to light and day-length, but it can respond to the rhythmic changes in these and sometimes this response is a negative one, producing SAD. By using extra light, the negative effect can sometimes be countered, even if this is just a temporary improvement. Therefore, it is possible that this debilitating condition can, for some sufferers, begin to be treated, at least partially successfully, with the right sort of light, and people can reclaim their lives.

A clear drawback to this research is the fact that it was a single case study and as such one should be cautious about making generalisations. It is possible that the results were due to a **placebo** effect – the fact that Pat expected to benefit from the light therapy might alone explain her recovery. Nevertheless, other research confirms the link between lack of daylight and SAD. For example, Booker and Hellekson (1992) found an incidence of about 9 per cent in Alaska. Alaska lies across the Arctic Circle and so will have very restricted day-length and also low quality of light through the winter months.

However, Feadda *et al.* (1993) found similar rates of SAD in a retrospective study of seasonal mood disorders in Italy, a Mediterranean country known for its sunshine both in summer and most of the winter! If SAD is also showing up there, this suggests there may be causes other than lack of daylight. It is possible that the Italian study was flawed insofar as it was retrospective and therefore memories may have been distorted. Of course, if there really is a significant occurrence of SAD in sunny countries then it may well be that this condition is far more complex than we think.

Treatment of SAD

Light therapy was once hoped to actually cure the SAD condition, but early experimental studies had very poor methodology so what appeared to have been improvements may have been unrelated to the therapy. They could have been due to experimenter expectations. Lamm (1994) has reported improved methodology in the 1990s but his overview of research does not show any clear pattern, though many experiments are interesting. For instance, Avery *et al.* (1992, 1993) have shown a positive response in improving mood using dawn simulation. This involves a device which gradually increases light intensity towards the end of the sleeping time whilst the participant is sleeping, mimicking natural dawn, and reaching a bright light level at the desired waking time.

The light pathway in the brain may also be linked to the neuro-transmitter serotonin (see Chapter 3). Treatment with SSRIs (selective serotonin reuptake inhibitors) has also shown an improvement in mood for people with SAD.

Shift work

Many industries depend on shift work to keep going 24 hours a day. We obviously want our doctors, nurses and other health professionals to be functioning at whatever hour we need them. And long-distance drivers and airline crew are often working through the night. Many manufacturing industries also want their plant in action continuously and it makes good economic and commercial sense. But even electronic machinery requires human attention, and a humanitarian,

economic and psychological concern has been whether humans cope
well with sleep rhythms being disrupted.

As mentioned in Chapter 3, our innate biological clocks are reset at
least daily by environmental stimuli known as *zeitgebers*. The most
powerful *zeitgeber* is light, and this puts the endogenous clock mechanisms in tune with the environment, our external world. Additional
zeitgebers include mealtimes and other markers of daily/nightly
routines, such as clocks striking the hour and music associated with
times of day. This can give rise to psychological difficulties if different
zeitgebers are in conflict, for instance if twilight and sounds of
evening come when someone is waking to start their 'day' because
they are working a night shift. We know that the innate rhythms of
metabolic rate and particularly body temperature are fixed and do not
vary with either *zeitgebers* or altered daily shifts. There could be
conflict between the brain trying to work to one rhythm and the body
to another. However, one cannot assume that all individuals will experience the same problems because, as Webb (1975) showed, some of us
are more alert in the morning and others in the afternoon, that is there
is a pattern of individual differences. In fact some of us work naturally at night (those students who stay up all night writing their essays)
whereas others prefer to work in the morning.

Evaluation

One problem with shift work could well be mild sleep-deprivation. It
could well be difficult to adjust to daytime sleeping even in a well-
darkened room when *zeitgebers* such as noises outside are a clear
indication of the local world being awake. Akerstedt (1985) showed
that people on shift work slept 1–4 hours less than when they could
sleep normally at night. He also showed that they had a particular
deficit in REM sleep. If REM sleep has a particular function then this
function would also show a deficit. This is discussed in the later
section on performance deficits.

Alleviating shift-work effects

Czeisler has conducted a considerable amount of research related to
shift work and found (Czeisler *et al.*, 1982) that it generally took
people 16 days to adjust to a new shift pattern. They also found that

people were less tired and adjusted more easily if their shifts were rotated with the clock rather than against it, in other words a system of early shifts, then later shifts, then night shifts and then back to early shifts again. This would be working with, not against, the innate 24.9-hour clock and lengthening the day, that is getting up later, progressively, which (as was said in Chapter 2) is less stressful than having to get up earlier. Czeisler *et al.*'s ideas were applied to a Utah chemical plant and workers there reported sleeping better, feeling much less tired on the job, and experiencing increased motivation and morale. Self-reporting is not empirical evidence as it is of course completely subjective, but the management also reported increased output plus fewer errors being made, so there was consensus that the new shift patterns were an improvement. Gordon (1986) reported similar improvements in a study in the Philadelphia Police Department.

A different approach to improving life on shift work was taken by Dawson and Campbell (1991), who arranged for people on their first night shift to work under a 4-hour pulse of very bright light. This seemed to help these people adjust better, as their body temperatures did not fall as much as expected during the night shifts. The hours of bright light might have partly at least reset their endogenous clocks.

Jet lag

Anecdotal evidence has long supported sleep disturbances, headaches and feelings of mental dullness when several time-zones have been crossed. This **jet lag**, as the effects are known, is a feature of aircraft crews' lives and an unwelcome effect of many businessmen and holidaymakers' trips. These effects do not seem to happen much if people travel from north to south or vice versa, thus staying in the same longitude and therefore the same time-zone. This means that if someone flies from Manchester, Glasgow or Belfast to Accra in Ghana they should not suffer from jet lag. Even though the flight will have lasted several hours, they are staying in the same time-zone and so there will be no inner 'time' conflict and they will have neither gained nor lost any hours.

Psychological knowledge about our innate clocks and *zeitgebers* suggests that jet-lag effects are the result of a mismatch between our inner psychological rhythms and the outer *zeitgebers*, the environmental cues. For instance, if one flew from Britain to New York, a city 5 hours behind us, and arrived at New York time 3 p.m., one's internal clock would be at 8 p.m. And when physiologically the body was winding down in preparation for sleep, in New York it would be late afternoon and the locals would be at their psychological circadian peak. So there would be inner 'time' conflict and this is what is believed to produce the symptoms and inappropriate feelings of jet lag.

Evaluation

Jet lag is known to be more severe when flying from west to east, for example the shorter route from Britain to Asia, than from east to west. The suggested explanation here is linked to our 24.9-hour clock. It seems that a phase delay – delaying or putting on hold our internal clock, for example by staying up later – is easier to accommodate to than a phase advance – making one's internal clock skip ahead, for example going to bed earlier. This explanation certainly fits in well with anecdotal experience – most of us know that it is far easier to stay up late at night and feel fine at the time than it is to wake up even one hour earlier in the morning and feel morning-bright!

Psychologists Schwartz *et al.* (1995) analysed the results of the USA baseball major league from 1991–3 and found that West Coast teams who had travelled east over three time-zones had significantly fewer wins than East Coast teams travelling three time-zones westwards. This ties in well with the extra difficulty in adjusting when moving eastwards, a feature of jet lag.

The stress brought on by changing time-zones and the difficulty sleeping could in itself be a factor in upsetting body clocks. Stewart and Amir (1998) found that rats which have been emotionally upset are not as good at resetting their innate clocks using light as the *zeitgeber* as rats who have not been emotionally stressed. Stewart and Amir suggested that emotional upsets could make the SCN less responsive to light. This could be a factor in humans as well, as many people find long-haul travel and its associated time-changes stressful. This could mean that such people take longer to accommodate to the new time-zones. It could also explain why some people do not seem to experience jet lag after a long journey – such people might be those who do not experience travel and changing time-zones as stressors.

This hypothesis could even be applied to shift work, as we know that not everyone has difficulties coping with this.

Psychologically and physiologically the way to minimise the effects of jet lag are said to be to keep well hydrated, to avoid alcohol and caffeine (which interfere with the brain's normal functioning), and to fit in with the local *zeitgebers*, for example having meals at the 'correct' time. Logically, this ought to make their adjustment to local time much more quick and easy but there are no empirical data on this.

There is also a treatment available in the USA and mainland Europe but not in Britain. This is the hormone melatonin (see Chapter 3) which is naturally secreted by the pineal gland in the brain. Melatonin is thought to make us feel sleepy and start to wind down. Anecdotal reports suggest it can be useful in resetting the endogenous clock if small doses are taken a couple of hours before local bedtime. No real evidence is available at the moment, but research studies are in progress and so far seem to be supporting this idea.

PMS (pre-menstrual syndrome)

The monthly menstrual cycle is a normal rhythm of women between menarche and menopause. But across all cultures there are some psychological fluctuations which occur in only some women. The all-cultural nature of these is an indication that the fluctuations have a physiological cause and are not the product of specific cultural beliefs or behaviours. Typical changes, known collectively as PMS, occur a few days before the menstrual bleeding and include feelings of great energy followed by great exhaustion (Luce, 1971), plus headaches, increased irritability, depression and for some people also visual disturbances and mental sluggishness.

Evaluation

Dalton (1964) correlated the PMS period with an increase in accidents, less achievement academically, suicides and crime. Though a correlation cannot actually infer causation, but just a possible link, in recent years PMS has been increasingly accepted by the legal world as a contributory cause of anti-social behaviour, with (in some cases) custodial sentences being reduced as a result. It is suggested that in some women the hormonal changes of their menstrual cycles adversely affect normal behaviour, but more research into PMS is needed to make clear conclusions possible and to clarify the continuum which has severe PMS as one extreme and no symptoms at the other.

Performance deficits

Errors or mistakes, known as performance deficits, have been linked with disturbances in our bodily rhythms, especially our sleep cycle. All of the above examples can be used as valuable comments on the psychological importance of our biorhythms.

Shift work, with its disruption of the daily rhythm, has the strongest links to performance deficits. Novak *et al.* (1990) studied accident rates in an industrial chemicals plant and found higher accident rates in shift workers compared to day workers. Gold *et al.* (1992) reported sleepiness and errors in nurses on shifts, supporting Hawkins and Armstrong-Esther (1978) who monitored eleven nurses on the first seven sessions of doing a night shift. They judged the nurses' performance to have reduced significantly on the first night, though this improved as the week went on. The sample was very small indeed and there was large variation in the results, but body temperature (which had been monitored as a measure of the innate biorhythm) had not adjusted by the end of the week.

Social data shows that motorway accidents are particularly likely to occur when the circadian rhythms are low, at 2–4 p.m., midnight to 2 a.m. and 4–6 a.m. Horne (1992) showed that a momentary falling asleep, sometimes for a few seconds only, was the probable cause, because an absence of skid or braking marks indicated that the driver had not been aware of the impending accident. This is likely to be because of a momentary lapse of consciousness, not of attention. He also found that these drivers were likely to have been awake for longer than usual, about 18 hours, and/or were sleep-deprived, as in shift workers.

All this has serious implications for our society. As stated earlier, it is normal to have many people working shifts – it is estimated that approximately 20 per cent of people employed in the United States work in shifts. Current psychological research suggests that many of them may therefore be under-performing at work, or before or after work. Some may be driving road vehicles or trains or planes. Some may be doctors or nurses or air traffic controllers, yet psychological research may not always be being applied to the performance of these vital roles. It will be expensive to improve people's working lives. In the early 1970s junior hospital doctors could be working a 100-hour week on duty. By the mid-1990s the weekly hours were down to 56 hours out of 72 hours on call in the hospital. The annual cost to the community of these changes has been in millions of pounds. But the hidden costs of not doing this, even in terms of performance deficits, would have been vast.

Summary

Most of us cope well with gradual changes in our rhythms, such as long days in summer and short ones in winter, but some people do seem more sensitive to these changes. When there is a discord between internal 'time' and external cues a person may experience negative effects, as in SAD (seasonal affective disorder), shift work and jet lag.

SAD is a depressive condition seemingly dependent on the quality and quantity of daylight. It is shown not only in inhabitants of the far north where there is little winter daylight, but also in Mediterranean countries, which suggests that there may be extra factors involved. Therapy uses light boxes and antidepressant drugs.

Shift work requires changes in a person's sleep–wake rhythm, so it is out of synchrony with the environment. Not everyone is badly affected by working through the night; those who are may be suffering from sleep deprivation. Research suggests that altering shifts by going forwards in time produces better adaptation than going backwards.

Jet lag affects aircraft crews and travellers. The disorientation after changing time-zones is worse when travelling from west to east rather than vice versa. Research suggests that the time-change itself is one factor, but that stress or emotion could be another.

The effects of disrupted bodily rhythms may also be observed in PMS (pre-menstrual syndrome). PMS is associated with fluctuations in mood and behaviour just before menstrual bleeding starts.

When bodily rhythms are disturbed, there may be associated performance deficits. Studies show that accidents frequently occur during night shifts when our circadian rhythms are low. This takes on extra importance when we consider some jobs, such as air traffic controllers, doctors and nurses.

For each of the conditions in this chapter – SAD, shift work, jet lag, PMS – refer back to the theories of sleep and of dreaming and make short notes to explain which theories tie in with each disorder.

Further reading

Green, S. (1998) Sleeping. *Psychology Review* 4 (3), February. (An excellent summary of the psychology of sleep.)

There are some really good websites which make interesting reading:

www.acep.org/POLICY/PR004166. (Website about circadian rhythms and shift work.)

www.mentalhealth.com (Has information about SAD and PMS.)

www.melatonin.com/ (Has more information about melatonin, SAD and sleep.)

8

Hypnotic states

Introduction

Hypnosis is a phenomenon which has been around for thousands of years – it's not modern, not 'New Age'! But we are now hearing much more about hypnosis – its possible uses by therapists in treating a variety of disorders or as a way to access buried memories. We also hear about hypnosis as a form of entertainment, both on television and on stage, and it can be very difficult to tease out what is factual or true and what is conjecture. The ancient Greeks used hypnosis, as did a Dr Mesmer in the eighteenth century in a series of so-called cures (it became known as 'mesmerism'). In recent years there has been a focus of research which is leading to a real increase in knowledge.

The hypnotic state

This state is induced only after the participant, client or patient has understood what is about to happen. It is said to be possible that someone could be hypnotised without their knowledge and therefore their consent, but this would be completely unethical and potentially dangerous. The hypnotist first suggests concentrating on some sort of small object or other target or else asks that the participant closes their eyes. Then suggestions of relaxation are made, perhaps associated with sleepiness or tiredness, for example 'you are feeling very, very sleepy' or 'your eyelids are so heavy they are closing'. The eyes close and, though under the lids eye movements can be seen in a similar way as in REM sleep, these people are definitely not asleep. Their EEG traces are similar to those of meditation or deep relaxation, not to those of sleep. It is likely that the parasympathetic part of the autonomic nervous system is activated and the sympathetic part inhibited to achieve this state. The heart-rate would slow, as would the breathing-rate. And blood would then be diverted to the internal organs and away from the skeletal muscles. This would contribute to the feelings of heaviness and warmth in the limbs, which are often suggested to the participants and known as **ideomotor** and **ideosensory** effects.

Features of the hypnotic state

About 90 per cent of the population can be put into a hypnotic state and will then show some of the characteristics listed below. The first three are the main characteristics of the hypnotic state and explain much of the behaviour associated with that state. In hypnotism stageshows people display this overall in what they do and don't do. They are quiet and passive until something is suggested. When they are told their arm is heavy, it drops. If told it is weightless it 'floats' upwards. If asked to describe the scent of a bottle of perfume they will use words such as 'flowery', 'sweet', 'lovely' – even if what they are smelling is a dilution of ammonia, bleach or vinegar. The remaining characteristics are additional possible features of the hypnotic state.

Narrowing of attention This means that the hypnotised person seems less aware of what is going on around them. For instance, if they are told to listen to only one voice or sound they apparently do just that and are unaware of any other voices or sounds. The paradox is that the person's brain is still receiving, analysing and processing all sensory information, not just the one sound or voice. This has been demonstrated by Miller *et al.* (1973) using the Ponzo perceptual illusion. In this, two parallel lines of identical length are shown, one a little distance above the other. Seen like this they are clearly of the same length. But when slanted lines like the two sides of a triangle are put surrounding the parallel lines, these no longer seem the same length: one appears to be shorter than the other, probably because the slanted lines provide distance cues (like railway lines disappearing into the horizon). This is shown in Figure 8.1.

But if hypnotised people are shown the full illustration with the four lines and then told that the two slanted outer lines have disappeared so they are not visible, these participants then still say the upper parallel line is longer than the lower one. In other words, these hypnotised people seem still to be processing the full information, that is perceiving all four lines even though they say they can see only two of them.

Distortion of information processing   Allied to the narrowing of attention is the acceptance by the hypnotised person of contradictory or nonsensical information such as oxymorons. Hypnotised individuals accept such statements whereas normally they would be rejected as impossible, stupid, or just plain silly. Another similar kind of behaviour would be behaving as a young child, complete with squeaky voice, after being told you are six years old.

Figure 8.1 **The Ponzo illusion**

Suspension of planning This describes the extreme passivity of hypnotised participants. They do not appear to react to their surroundings unless told to do so. They will remain sitting quietly until the suggestion is made actually to do an activity. They also will react to things which are in fact not present (a positive hallucination) as well as fail to react to things which are present (a negative hallucination). In stageshows hypnotised people often speak to imaginary others, after being told they are present in person, and avoid imaginary objects as they walk, after being told these exist. They will also try and walk through objects such as a table or chair if they are told there is clear space in front of them.

Post-hypnotic suggestion This is a strange feature where the hypnotised participant can be told that they will behave in a certain way when they return to their non-hypnotised awareness. This could involve reacting to an object or to a word or other sound. For instance, this is used in some types of addiction therapy, like suggesting that the participant will feel sick whenever they put a cigarette in their mouth. This would clearly discourage the smoking habit. Interestingly, following the implantation under hypnosis of such suggestions, when people are asked about this sort of response they will rationalise their behaviour and explain or justify it with sensible reasons. Those trying to lose weight who have had a strong desire for rich food may reach for a luscious cream cake, then draw back their hand saying that they know this would be unhealthy for them. Of course it is also possible, but unlikely, that they had come to this decision consciously!

Post-hypnotic amnesia It seems that if hypnotised participants are told that they will have no memory of whatever has occurred during the hypnotised state once they have 'woken up', then this in fact happens. They seem genuinely unaware – there is an amnesiac period. But if they are re-hypnotised then they are likely to recover those memories, a form of 'state-dependent' remembering (a description of state-dependent forgetting can be found in John Henderson's book *Memory and Forgetting*, also in this series). The hypnotic suggestion of amnesia seems able to insert some sort of block into the processing for retrieval of information.

Hypnosis and individual differences

As mentioned above there is about 10 per cent of the population who just don't seem to be able to enter the hypnotic state. Hilgard himself suggested a continuum for hypnosis with two extremes. At one end he reckoned that there are up to 10 per cent of the population who are highly resistant to hypnosis and at the other end are another group of up to 15 per cent who are extremely susceptible to hypnosis. The rest of the population, 75–80 per cent, come somewhere in between these two extremes (see Figure 8.2). A person's hypnotic susceptibility can be measured on the Stanford hypnotic susceptibility scale, shown on page 92.

The suggestions are worked through in order, from 1 to 12, until the point is reached where the participant does not comply with the suggestion. The level reached is their personal susceptibility on the scale. This sees hypnotic susceptibility not as being all or nothing but as a trait varying in strength from individual to individual. On stage, hypnotists start with suggestions for their volunteers to relax and then often work through some of these suggestions.

Whilst there is no special type or personality or other factor which explains this variation, there are some correlations with other personality traits, such as being imaginative and fantasy-prone. We just have to remember that correlations do not infer causality, only links. So the positive correlation between the above scale and susceptibility just flags up a relationship, not a cause-and-effect. Also, it seems, this relationship shows up only if people are expecting to be hypnotised, otherwise the correlation is not shown (Council *et al.*, 1986).

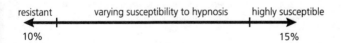

Figure 8.2 **The hypnosis continuum**

The Stanford hypnotic susceptibility scale

1   *Arm lowering*: A participant is told that their outstretched arm is getting increasingly heavier, the arm starts to fall.

2   *Moving hands apart*: When a participant's arms are stretched out straight in front and told that the hands repel each other, the two hands start to move apart.

3   *Mosquito hallucination*: The participant responds to a suggestion of an annoying mosquito buzzing round by trying to swat it away.

4   *Taste hallucination*: The participant agrees with suggestions of sweet and then sour tastes in their mouth.

5   *Arm rigidity*: After being told that an outstretched arm is getting more and more stiff the participant is unable to bend it.

6   *Dream*: The hypnotised participant is told they will dream about hypnosis, and then reports this happening.

7   *Age regression*: The participant acts in accordance with whatever younger age they are told, including suitable handwriting being produced.

8   *Arm immobilisation*: After being told that the arm cannot be lifted, the participant finds it is so.

9   *Anosmia (loss of smell)*: The participant becomes unable to smell household ammonia after being told it is odourless.

10 *Hallucinated voice*: The participant answers to an hallucinated voice.

11 *Negative visual hallucination*: After being told there are only two coloured boxes when there are three, the participant says only two are seen.

12 *Post-hypnotic amnesia*: Until a pre-arranged sign or signal is made, the 'awakened' participant cannot recall certain information given when hypnotised.

List the six features of the hypnotic state and, with each one, give two important points, for example:

Narrowing of attention: less aware, Ponzo lines

Theories of hypnosis

There are two main theories of hypnosis in mainstream psychology. One, the **state theory**, suggests that hypnosis is a special state of awareness. The other, **non-state theory**, takes the view that the hypnotic trance is merely a social role or placebo effect.

State or neo-dissociation theory

This theory suggests that the hypnotic state is a special process or dissociation of consciousness, that is a special state, and was proposed by Hilgard (1975, 1977). It is suggested that consciousness is divided into many separate mental channels, rather like the columns in a table, and under hypnosis these dissociate – that is they separate or move apart. So, though we are subconsciously still aware of what is going on all around us, we are focused on the hypnotist. Hilgard suggested a phenomenon he called the **hidden observer** – some part of the mind which could cross between the different mental channels and be aware of them, sample them and report on them. This is an adaptation of Descartes' seventeenth-century notion of a theatre of consciousness.

Experimental studies

In an early experiment Hilgard told a hypnotised participant that he was about to become temporarily deaf and would be able to hear only when a hand was put on his shoulder. Subsequently, this participant was asked to raise a finger if any part of him could still hear and, to everyone's surprise, he did so! Hilgard interpreted this as strong support for the existence of a hidden observer, and that this was the part of the mind which had heard the question and which had replied by raising the finger. (This research is reported in more detail in Chapter 9.)

A further set of experiments used a technique called the **cold pressor** test, in which a hypnotised participant is told to keep their hand or forearm in ice-cold water for as long as possible. This is actually very painful to do, as extreme cold can damage our living tissues and the pain is a warning (so there might be an ethical issue here). Most non-hypnotised people will only be able to keep their hand in the icy water for less than half a minute, but Hilgard's hypnotised participants who were told they would feel no pain lasted for an average of approximately 40 seconds. Interestingly, if these people were asked if they felt any pain they replied that they didn't; but if they were asked to write down their answer they wrote that they did feel a lot of pain. This was the hidden observer answering, according to Hilgard. The hypnosis had separated off the channel of consciousness which was reacting to the hypnotist, but the hidden observer had access to the other channels including those which perceived pain. It is of course possible that hypnosis might impart an actual temporary neural block within the brain or nervous system which would prevent some impulses from being transmitted and this could be Hilgard's dissociation, but this is hypothetical.

The experiment by Miller *et al.* (1973) with the Ponzo visual illusion can also be explained in terms of the hidden observer. It might be that the hidden observer, who could see all four lines, was influencing the judgement that the two lines were different in length.

Evaluation

All the above studies involved interpretations of behaviour and so are open to criticism of bias and subjectivity. Sarbin and Slagle (1972) pointed out that there is no reliable empirical method of distinguishing between the hypnotised and non-hypnotised states. However recent studies have used brain-scanning techniques to monitor what is and is not actually happening in the brains of hypnotised people. Spiegel *et al.* (1998) are reported to be working on hypnotised people using **PET (positron emission tomography) scans** to monitor changes in blood flow to areas of the brain. Blood flow correlates with activity, as the more energy brain cells are using the more blood will be required to supply glucose and oxygen. This Harvard research is still being analysed prior to publishing, but results seem to show that different areas of the brain are used when under hypnosis. One task under hypnosis was to 'become' colour-blind so that everything is seen in shades of grey. The participants who were able to experience this hallucination showed distinctly different PET scans from those who were not successful with the task. Some of the observed differences were in specific parts of the brain cortex, relevant to visual and imagination tasks. This seems like strong supportive evidence for a hypnotic state. Of course PET scans only measure blood flow, they do not tell us what people are thinking, only which areas of their brains are more or less active. So this is after all not firm evidence of a special, altered state.

The above criticisms also apply to research in Montreal, where Rainville *et al.* (1999) investigated hypnosis and pain-management. Many reports support the good effects of this application of hypnosis. The team researched only eight participants, who were hypnotised and then each told to put a hand into hot water. Some were then told the water was more unpleasantly hot, others that it was less hot. All eight participants accepted the given information and acted accordingly. PET scans showed that patterns of blood flow altered in a small area of the inner cortex which is involved in emotional perception (the anterior cingulate) and this correlated with what the participants were told and also with what they reported feeling.

On the other hand, Kirsch (1998) reports an older study of his where participants were secretly filmed whilst listening to a hypnotism tape. This was done twice, as a practice- or dummy-run when the participants were alone and again as the experimental- or real-run with an investigator present. Some participants behaved with more compliance to the tape when they knew they were observed than when they were alone. These he calls **'simulators'** and suggests they were pretending to be hypnotised. Others behaved the same in both conditions and Kirsch calls these **'reals'**, that is they were truly hypnotised. This is a good demonstration of hypnotism but unfortunately still does not answer the question as to whether or not it is an altered and special state of consciousness.

The non-state or placebo theory

This theory accepts that the hypnotic state involves relaxation, expectation, suggestibility, compliance and imagination. Barber (1969) suggested these factors contribute to the social role which the participants are playing, involving a suspension of personal control rather similar to getting involved in a fictional or fantasy video. His view is that the people and their abilities are special but the hypnotic state is not.

Spanos (1991) also suggested that by agreeing to be hypnotised the participant has entered into a form of contract, rather as paid participants are said to do in a psychology experiment. This social contract implies the hypnotism will be successful and that people will comply with the hypnotist's suggestions and instructions. In public performances there is additional social pressure to conform to the social norms of such a show and not spoil the entertainment.

Evaluation

Crawford and Gruzelier (1992) found certain specific changes in brain electrical activity during hypnosis and others have commented that the EEG traces of the hypnotic state are very closely similar to those of deep relaxation and meditation, in other words that the hypnotic trance is a form of deep relaxation. Council and Kenny (1992) found that experts could not tell the difference between two groups of self-reports, some from people in hypnotic induction and others from people having relaxation training, again suggesting that the two states are highly similar.

The above would appear to support the non-state theory, that is that hypnotic phenomena can all be explained in terms of other, normal behaviours. Additional support comes from interpretations of Gruzelier's (1998) review of research. His team's work at Imperial College uses scalp electrodes attached to hypnotised participants. This has shown alterations to the activity in the frontal lobes of the cortex – sites of thoughts, planning and imagination – when the hypnotic trance is induced. Though Gruzelier interprets these data as more than simple inattentiveness or relaxation, others still maintain this is no special altered state. This is still seemingly a matter of opinion not fact. One of Gruzelier's tests had hypnotised people doing a simple visual-cue test, based on colour perception. They had to alter their response when the cue colour changed. Hypnotised participants made far more mistakes than those non-hypnotised and the scalp recording showed that though the colour changes were being detected the hypnotised participants were not using this information to change their responses. Gruzelier suggested that hypnotised people lose interest in critically monitoring their perceptions and behaviours, and instead become far more credulous.

But is this an altered state? Wagstaff (1981, 1995) pointed out that the majority of people who have been hypnotised admit to having been role-playing or just plain pretending. Of course there is no way of knowing the truthfulness of these personal reports. Wagstaff himself was a participant in a stageshow of hypnosis as a 22-year-old student. He was not suggesting that hypnotism is a system of fakes and forgeries, but that it is not 'one' state. Wagstaff interprets hypnosis as an undefined behaviour varying in its make-up according to what the people involved want it to be. He says the changes in PET scans and scalp recordings under hypnosis are just reflecting the perfectly normal changes in concentration, relaxation and so on, in line with whatever instructions the participants have received. He supported this interpretation by referring to the successful use of hypnosis in pain-management. In this instance people are using their imaginations successfully to distract themselves from certain incoming unpleasant stimuli.

A final piece of support for the idea that hypnosis is non-state, that is not distinct from 'normal' behaviour, is from an older Kirsch (1997) study of expectation. Participants were exposed to faked hypnotic experiences, such as being told, during hypnosis, that colours or music would be experienced. These stimuli were in fact real, actual colours projected on a wall and music from a tape. The participants were led to believe the stimuli were hypnotic effects. After this experimental manipulation, the participants were found to have become more susceptible to being hypnotised – their expectations about hypnosis had been changed and therefore their compliance to hypnotic suggestion appears to have too. Of course nowadays this method would be considered unethical, as it involved deception and a lack of regard for the participants' psychological state.

Psychodynamic theory

One must not, of course, omit the psychodynamic approach to the hypnotic state. This regards the hypnotic trance as a special state of consciousness which gives an unique pathway into the unconscious. In Freudian terms the unconscious is a seething mass of our experiences, our psychosocial past, which is kept firmly out of our conscious minds. This is because the sum total of our experiences would be far too disturbing, producing deep anxieties and guilt. These buried memories can be a negative influence on our current selves, a threat to sanity or even to life when we are unconsciously influenced or driven by them. Psychotherapy aims to free, identify and neutralise such threats from the unconscious, and hypnosis is one technique used to pursue this aim, particularly where the threat is suspected to originate in early childhood.

Freud himself abandoned hypnosis after some time, as he felt he was hearing fantasies rather than true experiences from the past. However, Hart and Hart (1996) reported that it is in use currently as a means of freeing repressed memories of experiences which are blocking successful therapy. One strong note of caution here was sounded by Andrews (1997) who, after a careful overview of memories recovered under hypnosis and using other techniques, has advised extreme caution in accepting such recollections as reliable or factually correct. Loftus (1997) has written extensively on the unreliability of these **recovered memories** and is strong in her doubts of their validity. There is clear relevance here to the current child-abuse debate, where some evidence has relied on such recovered memories.

Conclusion

Almost all of us experience vivid dreams at some time or other, showing the brain is well capable of constructing fantasies and unreal experiences. We can also be caught out by visual illusions of many sorts. On the other hand there are stories about people able to endure major surgery with no pain relief other than hypnosis. What does this mean when related to the phenomenon of hypnosis? Well, opinion within psychology is fairly well polarised.

There are those, such as Spiegel, who say that our perceptions are complex amalgams of raw sensory input combined with what we already know, such as internal mental images, schema and scripts. Spiegel believes that hypnosis is a special state of focused concentration, a trance, which enables those hypnotised to experience unusual brain arousal and activity, such as distancing themselves from pain.

Others, such as Wagstaff, think that hypnotic phenomena are features of normal behaviour and not a special state. Hypnosis, they say, works best with those participants who have a rich and vivid imagination, and as they bring the skills from this into play for pain relief, for example, it is to be expected that their brain-scans and -activity alter. It would be most odd if they did not.

In other words, the research and the arguments go on and one must wait to see whether this emperor is, or is not, wearing his clothes.

Summary

The hypnotic state has been known for thousands of years. It is induced through deep relaxation and involves the activation of the parasympathetic division of the autonomic nervous system. Ninety per cent of the population can be hypnotised to some degree. There are five features of this hypnotic state: narrowing of attention, distortion of information processing, suspension of planning, post-hypnotic suggestion and post-hypnotic amnesia. The degree of hypnosis can be measured using the Stanford hypnotic susceptibility scale, which has twelve levels. Participants are taken through this scale of hypnotised behaviour until they no longer comply with suggestions.

The three theories of hypnosis are:

1   The state or neo-dissociation theory, which suggests a special and different state of consciousness which can be sampled by a 'hidden observer'. The experimental support is good but may be flawed.
2   The non-state or placebo theory, which does not see the hypnotic state as a special state of consciousness/awareness, but one in which participants role-play under a kind of social contract.
3   Psychodynamic theory, which strongly supports the idea of a special state of consciousness/awareness that gives unique insight into the unconscious mind, so that threats from the unconscious can be neutralised. Many psychoanalysts support its use in

freeing repressed memories. There is concern about the validity and use of such recovered memories.

For each of the three theories make a title of the theory's name and then bullet points as follows:
- The main research supporters and research study names (for example 'hand in cold water').
- Positive evaluation studies/comments.
- Negative evaluation studies/comments.

Further reading

Kline, P. (1994) Some psychoanalytic perspectives. *Psychology Review* 1 (2), 7–9. (A useful overview of psychoanalysis from one of the key figures in this area.)

McIlveen, R. (1995) Hypnosis. *Psychology Review* 2 (2), 8–12. (Valuable background reading at an accessible level.)

9

Study aids

IMPROVING YOUR ESSAY WRITING SKILLS

At this point in the book you have acquired the knowledge necessary to tackle the exam itself. Answering exam questions is a skill which this chapter shows you how to improve. Examiners have some ideas about what goes wrong in exams. Most importantly, students do not provide the kind of evidence the examiner is looking for. A grade C answer is typically accurate and reasonably constructed but has limited detail and commentary. To lift such an answer to a grade A or B may require no more than fuller detail, better use of material and a coherent organisation. By studying the essays presented in this chapter, and the examiner's comments, you can learn how to turn grade C answers into grade A. Please note that marks given by the examiner in the practice essays should be used as a guide only and are not definitive. They represent the 'raw marks' given by an AEB examiner. That is, the marks the examiner would give to the examining board based on a total of 24 marks per question broken down into Skill A (description) and Skill B (evaluation). Tables showing this scheme are in Appendix C of Paul Humphreys' title in this series, *Exam Success in AEB Psychology*. They may not be the marks given on the examination certificate received ultimately by the student because all examining boards are required to use a common standardised system called the Uniform Mark Scale (UMS) which adjusts all raw scores to a single standard acceptable to all examining boards.

The essays are about the length a student would be able to write in 35–40 minutes (leaving you extra time for planning and checking). Each essay is followed by detailed comments about its strengths and weaknesses. The most common problems to look out for are:

- Failure to answer the actual question set and presenting 'one written during your course'.
- A lack of evaluation, or commentary – many weak essays suffer from this.
- Too much evaluation and not enough description. Description is vital in demonstrating your knowledge and understanding of the selected topic.
- Writing 'everything you know' in the hope that something will get credit. Excellence is displayed through selectivity, and therefore improvements can often be made by *removing* material which is irrelevant to the question set.

For more ideas on how to write good essays you should consult *Exam Success in AEB Psychology* (Paul Humphreys) in this series.

Practice essay 1

Discuss research into factors involved in bodily rhythms. (24 marks)   [AEB 1999]

Starting point: One of the dangers in this part of the syllabus is that students present their 'sleep answer' no matter what the question is. In the case of this essay, a prepared sleep answer would receive little credit. However, the material could be used selectively to frame an appropriate answer to the question that has been set. More appropriate material exists and would need to be included to improve the quality of your answer. A good answer should represent the range of different kinds of bodily rhythms and, for each, provide description, empirical support and evaluation. The word 'research' in the title means that you can describe either theory or empirical studies, or both. Evaluation can be achieved by, for example, assessing alternative explanations, criticising research on methodological or ethical grounds and/or looking at applications of the research.

Much research has been conducted into the factors involved in bodily rhythms. Factors researched can be physiological, environmental or psychological.

There are many bodily rhythms which last a certain period of time. Circannual rhythms are those which last for a year. Examples of this are migrations of birds and the mating cycles of animals. These can be shown to be due to environmental factors, as birds and animals move towards warmth and plentiful food. In humans, a condition known as Seasonal Affective Disorder (SAD) is also circannual. This can lead to periods of depression in winter months, and can be seen as psychological because the bad winter weather does lead to depression. It can also be shown to be physiological, as the absence of sunshine leads to the chemical absence of melatonin, which makes us feel happier.

Infradian cycles last over 24 hours, for example the menstrual cycle of women which lasts 28 days. The physiological effects of a menstrual cycle can be dizziness, and abdominal pains a few days before menstruation. This indicates that it is biological factors which are involved in the bodily rhythm of menstruation. However, there are also psychological effects, such as mood swings and irritability. This is known as pre-menstrual stress, but not all women suffer from PMS. This shows that both a mixture of psychological and physiological factors are involved in infradian bodily rhythms.

Circadian rhythms last for 24 hours. Some people have been shown to be 'morning' types who reach their physical and psychological peak in the morning, whereas others are 'evening' types. There is physiological evidence for this, as people's hormone levels rise and fall during the day, giving rise to their change in their mood and aptitude. It is also possible again that the level of daylight which varies during the day can affect a person's physiological and psychological state. Research also shows, however, that there are psychological factors which influence whether a person is a 'morning' or 'evening' type. A person's aptitude throughout the day may depend on whether or not they feel better able to do things in the morning or evening, and what their personal experience and routines are.

Nocturnal rhythms are those which occur at night, that is, sleep cycles. Much research has been done into whether sleep is for physiological or psychological repair. One theory, namely the 'Restoration and Repair Theory' states that sleep cycles are necessary for the synthesis of neurochemicals which are used during the body's daytime functioning.

However, more research has been done to disprove this theory because although we need sleep (lack of sleep leads to dizziness and irritability, even death in animals), when we lose sleep it is not essential to catch up on all the sleep lost. So this shows that the nocturnal bodily rhythms and sleep cycles are influenced by physiological factors.

Here are also theories which state that we need to sleep and have sleep cycles for psychological health. Freud believed that we sleep in order to dream, and our dreams are a disguised form of our repressed sexual anxieties and conflicts. This is supported because our dreams do seem to have meaning, but many researchers do not believe that our anxiety and conflict need to be sexual. This indicate that our nocturnal bodily rhythms are also influenced by psychological factors.

Sleep cycles follow a pattern which involves five stages, and although these vary in length of time for each person, they are seen in all people. REM sleep appears to be necessary for both physiological and psychological health.

Both physiological and psychological factors are involved in bodily rhythms but it is not clear which are most important. It is probably true that both factors have a part to play in the function of bodily rhythms. Some researchers do move towards a more eclectic viewpoint, believing that psychological, physiological and environmental factors are involved. This can be seen clearly in Seasonal Affective Disorder where environmentally, the lack of pleasant weather is a factor as well as the lack of sunshine during winter. This is shown in the effectiveness of light therapy as a treatment but also counselling can help.

Examiner's comments

The student has presented a coherent essay, there is quiet reasonable elaboration and a nice sense of structure. This gives one a sense that the student is familiar with the material and has a reasonable understanding. The essay covers a good range of different kinds of bodily rhythms providing reasonable details for each. However, one could not describe the material as 'well detailed'. There are no specific studies cited nor are the details of such research recorded. Instead the student refers each time to 'evidence' in general.

In terms of evaluation, the same criticism can be applied – it lacks detail. For example, the students says: 'So this shows that the nocturnal bodily rhythms and sleep cycles are influenced by physiological factors' but it has not been made explicit how the preceding material does show this. The evaluation offered is rather repetitive, rather simply saying that the research shows that psychological and physiological factors are demonstrated.

The essay is not totally focused on the question set. The candidate, half way through, slips into their sleep essay and throughout fails to focus directly on the issue of the factors which cause bodily rhythms. This doesn't mean that all is lost but it does preclude the essay from getting top marks.

This essay would receive about 8/12 for description and around 6/12 for evaluation, making a total of 14/25, likely to be equivalent to a grade C or possibly a grade B.

Practice essay 2

Describe and evaluate research into dream states. (24 marks)
[AEB 1998]

Starting point: Again this is an essay which appears to tempt some students to write about sleep whereas it is clearly on dreams. A further difficulty is that candidates write about REM sleep, making the presumption that this is equivalent to dreams. In order to be creditworthy you must make a link between REM states and dreams.

The use of the term 'research' means that you could describe either studies or theories and use either studies and/or theories to evaluate what you have described! In other words, as long as you stay with material on dream states, and you organise your essay in a coherent manner, you should do well.

One danger may be that you know too much and try to cram it all in. The examiner looks for your ability to be selective and therefore it may be preferable to focus on a few theories and ensure that each is carefully described and evaluated. Remember that, for top-band marks, you need to present depth and *breadth. Select those theories which give you the opportunity to show breadth and detail.*

Candidate's answer

Dreaming occurs when we are at sleep. Therefore it might be helpful to start by looking at the stages of sleep. Sleep is an ultradian rhythm. We experience 5 stages (4 stages of NREM sleep and one of REM sleep) which we go through 5 or 6 times a night. Each cycle lasts about 90 minutes. In REM sleep we dream, though there is evidence that we also dream sometimes in NREM sleep. In REM sleep our brain is active but we are, in effect, paralysed.

There are many theories about dreaming or REM sleep though psychologists still don't really know why we dream. The first theory I am going to look at is Hobson's activation synthesis model. This theory is a physiological one because it tries to explain dreams in terms of physiological processes. The brain is active when we sleep, as I have already said, and this activation is similar to the brain waves when we are awake. The brain interprets these signals and we experience them as dreams. In other words the brain synthesises the activation. For example, you might hear a tap dripping when you are in REM sleep and this leads you to dream about rain. But this theory can't explain why we don't dream in NREM sleep.

Another physiological theory is called Oswald's Restoration Model. This is like some theories of sleep generally. It says that during REM sleep our body is replenishing important biochemicals which have been used up during the day. This might be used to explain why babies have more REM sleep than adults.

Another theory of dreams was suggested by Evans. He said that the brain has to shut down in order to update memory files otherwise it would get overloaded. This might explain why older people dream less. The dolphin who apparently does not have REM sleep has a huge cortex to hold all its unwanted memories. Dolphins also sleep one hemisphere at a time. But this may not be related to REM sleep.

From a psychological point of view Freud would suggest that the choices we make when manifesting our dreams are the result of our repressions and unfulfilled desires. This manifest dream would be the vehicle which the therapist would use to discover the latent dream content which would be the cause of any neurosis or anxiety that the dreamer may be suffering from.

The problem with Freud's theory is that it isn't based on any actual evidence. He suggested it on the basis of his experience with disturbed female patients and therefore it may not apply to normal people.

So we can see that there are many different theories about why people dream.

Examiner's comments

The student starts off on sleep and one fears that they may be on the wrong tack. Fortunately they quickly focus on dreams and make the all-important link between REM sleep and dreaming.

The answer is nicely constructed and, even though it is short, contains a reasonable amount of material. The candidate has described four theories of sleep, though each is rather limited and perhaps lacking in detail. The importance of detail is that it demonstrates how much understanding the writer has of a named theory. It is one thing to identify a theory but another to be able to explain it well.

The evaluation is thinner than the description, though the candidate has managed to embed the points of assessment at appropriate points in the essay which gives it a nice sense of discussion – description and evaluation, description and evaluation, and so on.

Some material has been included, such as the mention of dolphins, but not very effectively used. You must demonstrate the relevance of anything you state and not presume that the reader will be able to make the link for you. You certainly can't get credit for the work the examiner has to do on your behalf and you can't assume that the examiner will know what you intended.

How might you improve this essay? Clearly the theories could have been better explained and certainly more assessment could have been offered. Four theories would be quite adequate and probably advisable because of the 'depth–breadth trade-off'. If you try to write about too many theories this inevitably reduces the amount of depth you can offer for each and means lower marks for the lack of detail.

This essay would receive about 7/12 for description and around 5/12 for evaluation, making a total of 12/25, the likely equivalent to a borderline grade C.

Practice essay 3

Describe and evaluate any *two* theories of hypnosis.
(24 marks)   [AEB 1997]

Starting point: There are no tricks to this question. You are required to demonstrate your knowledge and understanding of two theories, and to offer evaluation of them. Evaluation can be presented in terms of commentary, interpretation (how the theory could be applied), alternative views/theories and/or empirical evidence which supports or attacks the theory. In other words there is no end to what you could use for evaluation. One useful 'trick' to remember is to use words such as 'So ...' or 'Therefore ...' or 'However ...'. Sentences starting with such words are likely to end up presenting evaluative material.

Candidate's answer

Hilgard believes that is a special and altered state of consciousness. He explained his theory using the concept of a 'hidden observer'. This is the idea that even when you are hypnotised one part of you is conscious and observing what is going on so that, when you 'wake up', even though you may appear not to know what was going on, the hidden observer does. Hilgard demonstrated this in an experiment where he hypnotised a person, inducing deafness in him. While the participant was in the hypnotic state Hilgard would ask him to raise his forefinger. If he was really deaf he couldn't do this, but to Hilgard's surprise he did raise his forefinger. So the unconscious hypnotised part was of the person's mind was deaf whereas another part remained unhypnotised. This conscious part is the hidden observer.

Hilgard used another test to demonstrate the hidden observer. This was the cold pressor test. A participant is asked to plunge their arm into icy cold water while hypnotised. They can stand the pain longer than someone who is not hypnotised which suggests that the brain is in some way blocking off the pain. If the hypnotist asks the hidden observer to rate the pain 'it' reports feeling more pain than the hypnotised part does!

Hilgard doesn't think that hypnosis stops pain but it makes it more tolerable. This can be used to explain why hypnosis is useful in dentistry or childbirth.

Barber put forward a different theory of hypnosis. He claimed it isn't a distinct state of consciousness, but instead it is just an example of someone playing out a social role. Barber's theory is called the non-state theory. It could be that people act like they are hypnotised because they know that is what is expected of them.

This is supported by the fact that some people are more easily hypnotised than others and this tends to be those people who believe in hypnosis.

Barber also demonstrated his theory using the human plank trick. In this experiment a hypnotised person lies across two chairs so that his body is seemingly magically suspended. Barber said that anyone can do this, you don't have to be hypnotised.

The hidden observer has also been criticised. It has been said that the participant was just following the hypnotist's instructions and brought the hidden observer into play when it was requested. The cold pressor test can also be explained in terms of expectations. People who think they will be able to withstand more pain when hypnotised are then able to stand more pain. Psychological research has shown what a powerful influence expectations can have on behaviour. For example, the self-fulfilling prophecy.

Examiner's comments

See if you can spot the evaluative comments. Is any empirical evidence offered to support either theory? Any applications? Any comments on the methodology? The answer is yes, some of these are present, but they generally lack detail and elaboration. What is here is relevant to the question set and demonstrates knowledge and understanding. However it is limited in terms of the amount of material presented (what we might called 'breadth') and the details (the 'depth'). The candidate has at best given us information about two studies (the hidden observer and cold pressor test) and used both as support for the theories presented. Other material is also offered as evaluation (using hypnosis to alleviate pain and to explain the human plank trick).

The candidate has not given us a very clear explanation of either theory, so that we might regard the descriptive side of the answer rather basic though it is generally accurate and reasonably constructed. The candidate has also used specialist terms which creates a sense of knowledge. Both the language and the general structure improve the quality of the answer because they suggest that the student was not presenting some rather half-baked ideas but had given the matter some thought and was able to present an organised and educated response. What was needed was just more of the same – more studies, applications, comments and more description of the theories themselves.

In total this answer would receive around 6/12 (description) and about 6/12 (evaluation) for a total 12/24, probably equivalent to a borderline grade C/D.

KEY RESEARCH SUMMARIES

Summary 1

'The relation of eye movements during sleep to dream activity: An objective method for the study of dreaming', W. Dement and N. Kleitman in *Journal of Experimental Psychology* (1957) 53(5), 339–46.

Introduction

Previous research had shown two types of sleep, one with the eyes still (called NREM sleep) and the other with the eyes moving rapidly under the closed eyelids. The rapid eye movement sleep, REM, seemed to be when dreams were occurring and this research set out to test this idea rigorously. Two other questions were considered. First, whether a correlation could be shown between time spent in REM and estimates of dream-length; second whether the type of eye movement occurring during REM sleep related to what was happening in the dream itself.

Method

Nine adult participants were used: seven males and two females. Typically each was asked to arrive at the sleep laboratory after a 'normal' day, having eaten as usual with the exception of abstaining from alcoholic or caffeinated drinks. These two substances could have affected their sleep.

Various electrodes were taped to the skin on the head, some near the eyes to record eye movements and some on the scalp to record brain electrical activity as EEGs. The participants then went to bed, as normally as possible, in a quiet, dark room. They were woken at various times during the night and asked if they recalled any dreams. In total, for all nine participants, 61 nights were slept under these conditions and they were woken 351 times, on average 5.7 times per night. The mean sleeping time per night was 6 hours.

REM sleep and dreaming

The participants were woken during REM sleep and at varying times when in NREM sleep. The stimulus to wake was a bell ringing near the bed, loudly enough to make sure they all awoke easily and quickly out of whichever type of sleep they were in. They then spoke into a recorder by the bed, in other words there was no influence by the experimenters. But sometimes when the participants were heard recording an experimenter might enter the room and question them. If participants recorded having dreamt but were not able to recall the dream-content then this was not counted as dreaming.

Results

The results showed a significant link between dream recall when woken from REM sleep compared to NREM sleep. The totals are shown in the table and figure below.

Type of sleep	Dreams recalled	No dreams recalled
REM	152	39
NREM	11	149

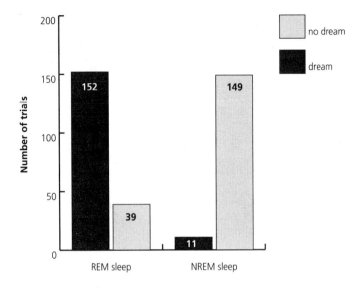

Histogram of dream recall in REM and NREM sleep

This clearly shows the difference between the two types of sleep. In addition, when woken from deep NREM sleep, participants seemed bewildered and reported varying emotions but no dreams.

Time spent in REM and dream-length estimates

In some of the trials participants were woken up either 5 or 15 minutes into an REM sleep period. They were then asked if their dream had been going on for 5 or 15 minutes. The figure below shows how accurate their estimates were. Although the participants were not asked to estimate the duration of their dreaming, but to choose either 5 minutes or 15 minutes, all but one were very accurate.

Type of eye movement and content of REM dream

Additional evidence was from observations of the directions in which the eyes of the participants moved during REM sleep. Some awaken-

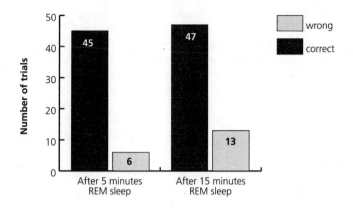

Histogram of accuracy of estimates of dream duration after 5 or 15 minutes REM sleep

ings were done after eyes had been moving either horizontally, vertically, moving around generally or not moving much. There did seem to be a link between the eye movements and the dream report. For instance, if the eyes were moving around generally then in the dream participants reported looking around for something; when the eyes were not moving much they reported looking at distant activity; some vertical eye movements were linked to dreaming about climbing a ladder whilst looking up and down, and one horizontal movement was linked to a dream of two people throwing tomatoes at each other!

Discussion

The conclusion from all this is that the study confirms that REM sleep is associated with dreaming and that most of our dreams occur in REM sleep. REM sleep occurs in separate episodes during the night's sleep and so dreaming too is presumed to be episodic. It is possible that the dream recall in NREM sleep is a memory of REM sleep dreaming.

Participants were able to judge the duration of their dreams accurately, though this was based on only a simple choice between 5 or 15 minutes. It would have been interesting to see the findings if they had been given a wider choice, say 1, 5, 10 or 15 minutes.

Eye movements did seem to fit in with the events of the reported dream, they were 'sensible' in their context.

Evaluation

This study formed the stimulus for many other sleep studies. As equipment has become more sophisticated so the knowledge of brain waves and brain-centre activity has increased. A problem common to many similar sleep studies has been the low ecological validity of the methods used. If we cannot expect to be able to measure or observe normal behaviour in abnormal surroundings, then it could be argued that we cannot expect to see entirely normal sleep and sleep patterns in the abnormal surroundings of a sleep laboratory, with wires taped to participants' heads.

More recent research has shown that eye movements in REM sleep are not closely linked (as this study suggested) to dream content, and that REM sleep deprivation is more damaging than loss of NREM sleep.

Summary 2

'A case study of long-term sleep deprivation', W. Dement in *Some Must Watch While Some Must Sleep*, San Francisco: W.H. Freeman, 1972.

Introduction

This case study was unique in that it was conceived, set up and run by the participant and not any researchers. In fact the researchers were so much not in favour of the procedure that they tried very hard to discourage the participant from going ahead.

In January 1959 there was a very lively and popular disc jockey (DJ) working in New York. He was Peter Tripp, and he ran highly successful radio and early television pop sessions: he is credited with inventing the concept of the 'Top 40' records and pioneered pop music on TV. He had read of attempts to do without sleep and was determined to set a world record for staying awake. Two hundred hours non-stop waking was his goal and he planned this as a charity stunt, but also wanted it to have more credibility. So he approached two young psychiatrists, Dr Louis (known as 'Jolly') West, now professor at UCLA, and Dr Floyd Cornelison, now professor at Jefferson Medical College, Philadelphia, and invited them to monitor his waking marathon for research. Neither of the young doctors were at all keen on Tripp's stunt. Both felt that he ran a great risk of long-term, maybe even permanent, damage. Indeed, Dr West in 1953 had gained experience in treating air force personnel returning after being captured in the Korean War – the setting for the M*A*S*H TV and film series. These war prisoners had been tortured and one technique used had been sleep deprivation. Even after debriefing and treatment these ex-prisoners did not feel themselves again and did not show the same personalities as they had before imprisonment. As a result of this experience Dr West felt sleep-deprivation experiments were too risky to do and were likely to lead to physical and mental problems.

However Peter Tripp insisted and, as he was clearly determined to carry out his stunt, aiming for 200 hours awake continuously, Dr Cornelison and Dr West decided to take the opportunity and monitor Tripp during this period. Their care included ensuring that Tripp underwent a full medical every day to check his general physical health.

Method

The waking stunt started on 20 January 1959 and Tripp broadcast his shows from a studio right on Times Square in the centre of New York. He was full of enthusiasm and tremendously well motivated, even describing himself as 'mother's little curly-haired boy'! He smiled and joked and showed his normal, bouncing, happy personality. He was watched all the time, whether or not he was broadcasting, and a Polaroid photo was taken each hour as a visual record.

Results

This initial positive attitude lasted for the first couple of days, but by the third day he was showing signs of great tiredness. He began to abuse people verbally and was so unpleasant to his regular barber who came in to shave him each morning that the man fled in tears never to return. After 87 hours awake Tripp admitted to feeling very tired and very sleepy. He was not allowed the opportunity to cat-nap even when he went to the lavatory, as someone was always with him to ensure the awake state was not interrupted.

As time went on the main *physical* change was that Tripp's body temperature started to fall. He began to feel cold all the time and took to wearing his coat and then a hat as well indoors. As his temperature fell his behaviour started to become quite bizarre. He started to have visual hallucinations, once mistaking a man who came into the studio for an undertaker come to bury him. Tripp rushed out of the studio, terrified, and ran right out into the street and into heavy traffic. He was caught unharmed, restrained and brought back, but wanted to continue his waking stunt.

By Day 5 Tripp was really losing his grip on reality. He developed auditory as well as visual hallucinations; his EEG traces were slowing down, showing that brain activity was also reducing. Every 90 minutes his hallucinations became worse for several minutes. This could have paralleled his sleep cycle with the hallucinations coming when REM sleep periods would have happened and quietening down when NREM sleep was due. In fact, the hallucinations could have been waking dreams and nightmares, Cornelison suggested. Tripp started to talk about seeing giant spiders crawling out of and over his shoes and other unpleasant perceptions were reported, but interestingly these symptoms always disappeared when it was time for him to put out his radio show. Dr West described Tripp as 'clearly psychotic' and reported that Tripp was not even sure whether he was himself or his own impostor at times.

As the waking period approached the 200-hour deadline the two doctors became so concerned that they considered stopping this marathon stunt. But they admitted that they did not want to spoil Tripp's achievement, especially when he was close to his goal, so they continued to monitor him. On the last evening they noted that as Tripp was walking around his EEG patterns were definitely those of sleep, not waking, even though his eyes were open, and he could walk and talk.

On 28 January Peter Tripp reached his target and broke the world record for sleeplessness. He had been awake for 201 hours in total. Of course, he then went to bed – and slept for 24 hours non-stop. EEG traces showed that most of those hours were spent in REM sleep. After this he woke to find his delusions gone and he felt back to

normal. Unfortunately, he subsequently showed a continuing personality change and his nature became argumentative and difficult. His
family life broke up, he was divorced and he even lost his DJ job. He
became a salesman and travelled around, drifting from town to town
and job to job.

Discussion

West and Cornelison now say they feel their work with Tripp was
dangerous: they did not face up to the possible consequences and
believe they should have thought again before agreeing to cooperate
with Tripp.

It seems that this and other sleep-deprivation studies have shown
that we can tolerate a varying amount, sometimes a considerable
amount, of loss of sleep without very serious ill effects. However,
prolonged sleep deprivation can, as in this case, have serious and
apparently permanent negative effects. Therefore, though we can
conclude that it is possible for us to function without sleep for some
time, it must also be said that sleep does seem to be essential for
normal behaviour.

Summary 3

'The "hidden observer" in hypnosis', E.R. Hilgard in *Divided
Consciousness: Multiple controls in human thought and action*, New
York: Wiley-Interscience, 1977.

The first appearance of a 'hidden observer'

This is a collection of studies illustrating the key concept of the
'hidden observer', first hypothesised by Hilgard in 1977.

The discovery of the 'hidden observer' phenomenon was quite
accidental and dramatic. Hilgard was teaching a class of students and
was using an experienced participant in a demonstration of the technique of hypnosis and the hypnotic trance. This participant was
actually biologically blind. In the trance state Hilgard told the participant that he would become deaf and would be able to hear normally
only when a hand was put on his shoulder. In this hypnotic state he
seemed deaf, seemed not to be aware of anything going on around

117

him. Hilgard demonstrated this and then questioned whether he was as unaware as he seemed. Quietly Hilgard asked him if there was any part of him which could still hear. If there was, would he please hold up a finger. To everyone's amazement the man raised his finger! The participant then wanted to know what was going on, so Hilgard put a hand on his shoulder so he could hear and said he would explain later, but also asked the man if he would explain what he knew of what had been going on. The reply was that he had become deaf and was actually rather bored so he had started to think about a problem he was having in his studies – in fact a problem with statistics, like so many students. Then he felt his finger rise but did not know why. He wanted an explanation. Hilgard then spoke to the part of the man 'who had listened to me before and made your finger rise'. He also told the man what this part of him would say. This strange other part showed he had heard all of what had been going on and could and did report it. Hilgard coined the term 'hidden observer' to describe this aware part of the hypnotised person's mind.

Subsequent research

Many further experiments have supported the existence of the hidden observer, particularly in studies involving perception of pain. In these the hypnotist may suggest the pain will fade away and the participant reports that this is so, but when the hidden observer is asked they say the pain can still be felt, though often they report it as less than when they were not hypnotised.

Other studies have asked the hidden observer to write down answers to questions. This is often called automated writing and the written answers are often very different from what the hypnotised person is actually saying. Hilgard cites this as more evidence for the hidden observer and has compared this phenomenon to the everyday behaviour of dividing attention between tasks. For example, walking along whilst chatting to someone or driving a car and looking ahead as well as into the mirrors whilst steering. On the other hand, other researchers point out that the social contract implicit in hypnosis could produce compliance which itself might give these hidden observer results (Spanos, 1991).

Evaluation

One problem which Hilgard and his supporters have found is that not all hypnotisable participants have been able to demonstrate the hidden observer. This may be linked to an inner perception in these participants which is spontaneous and not suggested. It may be an example of individual differences. Those who do have a demonstrable hidden observer also are very susceptible to age regression under hypnosis: they easily feel and behave like children. But those who do not show a hidden observer do not find it so easy to regress in age as they seem always aware of their real age, so they experience a duality of themselves as they really are as well as themselves when much younger. This ability to be extra aware of themselves may prevent the formation of what is called the hidden observer.

Applications

This hidden observer phenomenon has been of great interest applied to the field of pain-management. It can be used for hypnotic **analgesia**, that is hypnotically induced pain reduction. Hilgard suggests that the pain can be separated from conscious awareness by an amnesia-like barrier and that this dissociation is not a conscious process. It seems to happen automatically as a result of the analgesic suggestion when hypnotised, but is restricted to those patients who are hypnotically responsive.

Evidence is based on experiments which used hypnotised people who were subjected to pain stimulation and were then asked to give a spoken assessment of how much pain they felt. Usually they were told that the affected limb had become numb, insensitive and they were asked to rate the pain on a numbered scale by pressing the appropriate numbered key. Generally speaking the hypnotised person gave a lower rating for pain than did their hidden observer. This technique has obvious very useful applications for people with chronic pain. However, Spanos (1986) quotes Wagstaff as saying that there are social psychological explanations for coping with pain and there is therefore no need to propose a special state of consciousness. It is sufficient to say that a response to hypnotic suggestion is goal-directed social behaviour.

However, this does not reduce the usefulness of the analgesia.

Gibson and Heap (1991) reported a case study of a woman with chronic pain of a burning sensation in her temples and ears which was worse in the evenings. She was not particularly susceptible to hypnosis and yet through hypnosis she was taught a technique to impose a fantasy upon her pain. She visualised lying on a warm, sunny beach with the sun's heat substituting for the pain and the pain locus moving from her head to her abdomen. After seven weeks practice she reported her level of pain as lower and she was taking fewer painkillers. A follow-up a year later showed that though the condition had not disappeared it had periods of remission and she seldom needed to use painkillers. Hilgard suggests that the pain in such cases is felt as happening to some other person, this being the hidden observer.

This was illustrated by another case study based on his work. A young woman of 30 with painful arthritis was not responding to hypnotic amnesia, but then the technique of dissociating herself from the pain was tried. She was able, under hypnosis, to view herself as if she were a bystander and was aware that although her body was in pain she was not concerned as the pain seemed to belong to someone else. Hypnotic training improved her ability to dissociate from the pain, to give it to the hidden observer in a way, and had some success in providing relief, especially when she was at home.

Glossary

The first occurrence of each of these terms is highlighted in **bold** type in the main text.

activation–synthesis theory The suggestion by Hobson and McCarley that dreams are the brain's attempts to make a narrative sequence out of its random firings when we sleep.

active sleep Sleep where brain activity is high, namely REM sleep.

adenosine A chemical, present in all living cells, which bonds with three phosphate groups to form adenosine triphosphate or ATP, which acts almost as cellular electric batteries to supply the cell with energy.

alpha waves These are brain waves recorded from someone who is awake and relaxed.

analgesia A term meaning pain relief. Analgesics are substances which provide pain relief, such as aspirin.

autogenic This refers to a condition or state initiated or originated by oneself, internally in the mind.

autonomic nervous system This is part of the peripheral nervous system (that is, nerves) which controls much of our involuntary behaviour, such as our heart-rate, breathing-rate and blood pressure.

biological clock An innate (that is, inherited) mechanism, probably in the brain, which acts to switch on or off certain behaviours or rhythms.

brain wave This is a pattern, recorded from the scalp, of the sum of the electrical activity in the brain. It is recorded as a graph of wave-like patterns. *See also* electro-encephalogram (EEG).

cerebellum Part of the hindbrain, the oldest and most basic part of the brain which keeps us alive. The cerebellum controls coordination and balance.

circadian rhythm A regular repeating pattern with a 24-hour cycle, for example the 24-hour sleep–wake cycle.

circannual rhythm A regular pattern with an annual cycle, for example hibernation in a squirrel.

cognitive vigilance This refers to our ability to pay attention to cognitive tasks such as problem-solving.

cold pressor A test used to assess the degree to which someone is hypnotised.

collective unconscious Jung's concept of a vast well of memories from all humanity, stretching back to earliest times, of which we are not aware but into which we can connect when dreaming.

coma A deeply unconscious state, where the person seems completely unaware of their surroundings and from which it is very difficult to be roused.

connectionist A concept from computer models of the brain which focuses on the importance of brain connections (that is, the synapses): how many there are, where they are, how complex the patterns of information flow within them are, and so on.

conscious The conscious mind is usually taken to mean all that we are aware of whilst awake, including being aware of ourselves, our emotions and thoughts, and so on.

core sleep Horne's concept of the part of sleep which is essential for normal functioning.

corpus callosum The wide band of nerve fibres which runs between the two cerebral hemispheres. It is the 'information highway' connecting the two halves of the brain, so each is aware of what is going on in the other half.

ecological validity This concept refers to the degree to which an investigation or its results relate to the real or natural world, that is to what extent its findings can be generalised to other situations. Low ecological validity could be where a laboratory investigation had been done. As a laboratory is not a normal setting for most people, we would count the ecological validity as low because one could not expect to see people's normal behaviour in such an abnormal setting.

electro-encephalogram (EEG) The record or trace of brain waves as measured from electrodes taped to a person's head and scalp.

endocrine system The system of glands which secrete hormones, including the pituitary gland, the pineal gland and the testes (*see also* hormones).

endogenous This refers to something which is within, or formed within, the body.

evolutionary theory One of the models suggesting an explanation of why sleep is necessary. The main assumption is that sleep evolved to perform an adaptive function, that is one which should promote survival and reproduction.

forebrain The most advanced part of the brain. It includes the hypo-thalamus and thalamus, the limbic system and the two cerebral hemispheres (or cortex).

growth hormone One of the hormones secreted by the pituitary gland in the forebrain. It is released mainly at night and influences both growth and repair in the body.

hallucinatory images Visual images which are perceived under various conditions including hypnosis, but which do not actually exist outside the mind of the perceiver.

hibernation A cyclical period of deep rest, usually during winter, in which the animals concerned minimise their energy-use and so are more likely to survive until conditions become more clement in spring.

hidden observer The concept suggested by Hilgard to explain that part of our consciousness which is not affected by the hypnotic state and so can observe and report on what is experienced by the other, separated, parts of consciousness.

hormones Chemical secretions made by endocrine glands. They pass directly into the bloodstream which transports them to their sites of action. They can be regarded as chemical messengers.

hypnogogic state The state characterised by deep relaxation and calmness. It is found in meditation and various relaxation programmes and also in Stage 1 of the states of sleep.

hypnosis The induction of either a special state of awareness, as argued by state theorists and psychodynamic theorists, or of a particularly compliant and suggestible state, as put forward by the non-state theorists.

ideomotor These effects refer to feelings about the body, such as that muscles or limbs have become very heavy when there has been no additional weight put on them.

ideosensory This refers to sensory feelings, such as of warmth spreading along the limbs when they are not being heated or insulated.

individual differences This is a fairly modern concept in psychology of the natural variation found amongst human populations in a number of factors or behaviours, including genetic make-up, personality, how much sleep they need, personal dream recall, intelligence and so on.

infradian rhythm A regular, repeating pattern with a cycle which is longer than 24 hours, for example, the human monthly menstrual cycle.

innate This means inborn, usually genetically inherited.

internal clock *See* biological clock.

introspection A technique for investigating the mind that was popular in the nineteenth century. It was based on people reporting their own thoughts. It fell out of favour when the behaviourist approach became popular, as introspection was seen as non-scientific and unreliable.

jet lag This term describes the mixed negative effects experienced by many people when they cross two or more time-zones and have to adapt to fit the new time they are in, for instance after flying.

latent content A term that was used by Freud for the hidden meaning of dreams. This was usually interpreted as wish-fulfilment.

locus coeruleus This small area of cells lies in the pons, next to the medulla in the hindbrain. It produces neurotransmitters, including noradrenaline which is associated with REM sleep.

manifest content A term used to describe the overt content of a dream, that is what is recalled.

melatonin A hormone concerned in the control of sleep periods. It is synthesised and secreted by the pineal gland.

menarche A term describing the onset of the menstrual or monthly periods during adolescence.

menopause Refers to the cessation of the menstrual or monthly periods during late middle-age.

menstrual cycle The cycle in the human female lasting approximately 28 days, which starts at menarche and continues monthly, unless interrupted by a pregnancy, until the menopause.

metabolic rate The rate of energy turnover or use in a living organism or cell.

micro-sleep Minute cat-naps or very small instants of sleep during awake periods; the instants of micro-sleep are so short-lived that the person is not aware of them.

migrations Cyclical, seasonal movements of animals between two locations.

nerve impulses Minute pulses of electrical energy which pass along neurones like tiny waves of electricity and which are the 'messages' conducted by the neurones.

neurochemical theory In the context of this book, this is one model which explains why we sleep. It can be considered a development of the restoration theory of sleep and suggests that both REM and NREM sleep are needed for the resynthesis of neurochemicals.

neurones Highly specialised cells which make up our brain cells and our nerves.

neurotransmitters These are one type of neurochemical, used to transmit nerve impulses from one neurone to the next, like a temporary chemical connecting bridge.

non-state theory The theory of hypnosis which explains hypnosis and the hypnotic state as a combination of expectation and suggestion and compliance, but not as a special altered state of awareness. (*See also* state theory.)

noradrenaline pathway This describes any pathway of neurones in the brain which are linked by the neurotransmitter noradrenaline. One such pathway is suggested to be vital for REM sleep.

ovarian hormones The hormones secreted by the two ovaries, the main ones being oestrogen and progesterone.

oxymoron This means a direct contradiction, often an impossibility, such as 'the mother was a man'.

paradoxical sleep A term that has been used to describe REM sleep because of the paradox or apparent contradiction between the highly active brain and the highly inactive body during this stage of sleep.

parasympathetic nervous system This is the division of the autonomic nervous system which, when activated, makes us 'rest and digest', that is calm down, slow down and relax. (*See also* sympathetic nervous system; autonomic nervous system.)

PET (positron emission tomography) scans A non-invasive imaging technique, which is able to produce detailed pictures or scans showing which regions or areas of the brain are active at any time.

pheromones Chemicals, produced and secreted into the air for transport to other animals of the same species. They do not have a scent, but are breathed in through the nose, absorbed and then travel in the bloodstream, usually to the brain, where they influence behaviour. Many pheromones have a reproductive function.

pineal gland This tiny gland lies in the cortex near the surface. It seems to be sensitive either directly, as in birds, or indirectly, as in humans, to daylight. It produces the hormone melatonin when dusk falls.

placebo A substance or procedure which has no real effect, that is it is a dummy. However, such placebos do seem to influence behaviour, perhaps by expectation, and this is called the placebo effect.

pons This is part of the hindbrain. It is a swelling of mainly nerve fibres near the medulla and contains small groups of nerve cells, some of which have a function in the control of sleep.

pre-conscious A sub-division of the mind on the fringes of what we are aware of, the fringes of consciousness. We are able to switch our attention to factors in the pre-conscious if we become aware of them, but until then we remain unaware of their existence.

quiet sleep Sleep in which we do not dream much, therefore the amount of brain activity is relatively quiet.

raphe nuclei A small groups of cells in the hindbrain near the pons. They are involved in the control of sleep. Serotonin, made from melatonin, accumulates in these nuclei before we go into NREM sleep.

RAS (reticular activating system) An important part of the mid-brain which links the hindbrain and forebrain. The RAS monitors what goes up and down between the forebrain and hindbrain, and closes down some channels when we go into REM sleep, thus producing the paralysis of the body.

'reals' This term refers to those people who, after hypnosis, are truly in a hypnotic trance. (*See also* 'simulators'.)

recovered memories These memories are ones the person was not aware of having until after some sort of intervention or therapy, for instance hypnosis. Recent advice from the Royal College of Psychiatrists (1998) advocates extreme caution before accepting such memories as factually correct.

REM-rebound effect This is the temporary increase in the proportion of REM sleep following sleep deprivation where REM sleep has been lost.

restoration theory This model suggests that we sleep in order to restore ourselves physically and psychologically, after the day's experiences, in preparation for the next day.

rhythm A regular, recurring pattern; in this context a pattern of behaviour or of changes in brain activity.

rhythmic firing pattern This refers to a regular rhythm in the pattern of working of a neurone or group of neurones.

SAD (seasonal affective disorder) A depressive type disorder of varying strength striking people in autumn and usually lifting in spring. It seems to be light related.

SCN (supra-chiasmatic nucleus) A tiny group of neurones lying above the point where the two optic nerves meet and partially cross over. It is highly significant in the control of the sleep-wake cycle and is probably the seat of one of our biological clocks.

serotonin This is an important brain neurotransmitter with several functions, including being involved in the control of sleep, especially NREM sleep.

'simulators' According to Kirsch (1998) these are people pretending to be hypnotised. (*See also* 'reals'.)

sleep deprivation This means deliberately being deprived of sleep. It could refer to losing all sleep, some REM or some NREM, or some of each sort of sleep.

sleep spindles These are particular patterns recorded on an EEG trace when someone is in Stage 2 NREM sleep.

split-brain procedure A surgical procedure to help epileptic patients. It involves cutting the corpus callosum and therefore separating the two cerebral hemispheres. Psychological investigations of these people provided valuable knowledge about the different functions of the two hemispheres.

state theory A theory of hypnosis that suggests that the hypnotic state is a different and special state of awareness, unlike any other awareness state.

stress This is usually regarded as an individual response to negative aspects of a person's environment, for example anxiety, fear, unpleasant stimuli. Too much stress has ill effects on most people.

sympathetic nervous system The division of the autonomic nervous system that stimulates the body to 'fight or flight', that is to prepare for sudden action. Among the effects are faster heart- and breathing-rates, and more glucose in the blood. (*See also* parasympathetic nervous system; autonomic nervous system.)

synapses The junctions between neurones where they come very close together but never actually make contact. There is always a synaptic gap between them.

thalamus A lower part of the forebrain which relays sensory impulses up to the cortex.

theta waves EEG patterns characteristic of REM sleep and dreaming.

ultradian rhythm A regular pattern with a cycle of less than 24 hours, for example, the NREM/REM sleep cycles in a night's sleep.

unconscious Freud's concept of a great hidden mass of negative memories, emotions and thoughts which have to be kept out of our conscious minds to preserve our sanity. Like many ideas it is, of course, hypothetical.

unipolar depression Also called 'clinical depression', this condition is characterised by a long-term low mood and associated difficulties, for example lack of motivation and concentration, loss of interests and pleasures, and thoughts of death.

zeitgeber An environmental factor (for example, light) which can act as a time-cue.

Bibliography

Akerstedt, T. (1985) Adjustment of physiological circadian rhythms and the sleep–wake cycle to shiftwork. In Folkard, S. and Monk, T.H. (eds) *Hours of Work*. Chichester: Wiley.

Alvarez, A. (1995) *Night: An exploration of night life, night language, sleep and dreams*. London: Cape.

Andrews, B. (1997) Danger of misleading. *The Psychologist* 10 (4), 153.

Arkin, A.M., Toth, M.F., Baker, J. and Hastey, J.M. (1970) The frequency of sleep-talking in the laboratory among chronic sleep-talkers and good dream recallers. *Journal of Nervous and Mental Disease* 151, 369–74.

Aschoff, J. (1965) Circadian rhythm of a Russian vocabulary. *Journal of Experimental Psychology: Human learning and memory* 104, 126–33.

Atkinson, R., Atkinson, R.C., Smith, E.E. and Bem, D. (1993) *Introduction to Psychology*. New York: Harcourt Brace Jovanovitz. 11th edition, pp. 238–9.

Avery, D.H., Bolte, M.A., Cohen, S. and Millet, M.S. (1992) Gradual versus rapid dawn simulation treatment of winter depression. *Journal of Clinical Psychiatry* 53, 359–63.

Avery, D.H., Bolte, M.A., Dager, S.R., Wilson, L.G., Weyer, M., Cox, G.B. and Dunner, D.L. (1993) Dawn simulation treatment and winter depression: A controlled study. *American Journal of Psychiatry* 150, 113–17.

Barber, T.X. (1969) *Hypnosis: A scientific approach*. New York: Van Nostrand.

Binkley, S. (1979) A timekeeping enzyme in the pineal gland. *Scientific American* 204 (4), 66–71.

Blackmore, S.J. (1988) A theory of lucid dreams and OBEs. In Gackenbach, J.I. and LaBarge, S. (eds) *Conscious Mind, Sleeping Brain: Perspectives on lucid dreaming*. New York: Plenum.

Blackmore, S.J. (1996) *In Search of the Light: Adventures of a parapsychologist*. New York: Prometheus Books.

Blakemore, C. (1988a) *The Mind Machine*. London: BBC Publications.

Blakemore, C. (1988b) Rhythms of life. Programme 4 in the BBC television series.

Bloch, V. (1976) Brain activation and memory consolidation. In Rosenzweig, M.A. and Bennet, E.L. (eds) *Neural Mechanisms of Learning and Memory*. Cambridge, MA: MIT Press.

Bollani, L., Dolci, C., Montaruli, A., Rondini, G. and Caran, F. (1997) Temporal structure of body core temperature in twin newborns. *Biological Rhythm Research* 28 (1), 29–35.

Booker, J.M. and Hellekson, C.J. (1992) Prevalence of SAD in Alaska. *American Journal of Psychiatry* 149, 1176–82.

British Psychological Society (1990) *Ethical Principles for Conducting Research with Human Participants*. Leicester: British Psychological Society.

Carlson, N.R. (1986) *Physiology of Behaviour*. Boston: Alleyn and Bacon. Third edition.

Cherry, E.C. (1953) Some experiments on the recognition of speech, with one and with two ears. *Journal of the Acoustical Society of America* 23, 915–19.

Clay, R.A. (1997) Meditation is becoming more mainstream. *American Psychological Association Monitor*, September.

Colquhuon, W.P. (1970) Circadian rhythms, mental efficiency, shift work. *Ergonomics* 13 (5), 558–60.

Coren, S. (1996) *Sleep Thieves*. The Free Press.

Council, J.R. and Kenny, D.A. (1992) Expert judgements of hypnosis from subjective state reports. *Journal of Abnormal Psychology* 101, 657–62.

Crawford, H.J. and Gruzelier, J.H. (1992) A midstream view of the neuropsychology of hypnosis: recent research and future directions. In Fromm, E. and Nash, M.R. (eds) *Contemporary Hypnosis Research*. London: Guildford Press.

Crick, F. and Mitchison, G. (1983) The function of REM sleep. *Nature* 304, 111–14.

Czeisler, C.A., Moore-Ede, M.C. and Coleman, R.M. (1982) Rotating shift work schedules that disrupt sleep are improved by applying circadian principles. *Science* 217, 460–3.

Dalton, K. (1964) *The Premenstrual Syndrome*. London: Heinemann.

Dawson, D. and Campbell, S.S. (1991) Time exposure to bright light improves sleep and alertness during simulated night shifts. *Sleep* 14, 511–16.

Dement, W. (1960) The effect of dream deprivation. *Science* 131, 1705–7.

Dement, W. (1972) *Some Must Watch While Some Must Sleep*. San Francisco: W.H. Freeman.

Dement, W. and Kleitman, N. (1957) The relation of eye movements during sleep to dream activity: An objective method for the study of dreaming. *Journal of Experimental Psychology* 53 (5), 339–46.

Dement, W. and Wolpert, E. (1958) The relation of eye movements, bodily movements and external stimuli to dream content. *Journal of Experimental Psychology* 55, 543–53.

Empson, J. (1989) *Sleep and Dreaming*. London: Faber and Faber.

Empson, J. (1993) *Sleep and Dreaming*. Hemel Hempstead: Harvester Wheatsheaf. Revised second edition.

Evans, C. (1984) *Landscapes of the Night: How and why we dream*. New York: Viking.

Feadda, G.L., Tondo, L., Teicher, M.H., Baldessarini, R.J., Gelbard, H.A. and Floris, G.F. (1993) Seasonal mood disorders: Patterns of seasonal recurrence in mania and depression. *Archives of General Psychiatry* 50, 17–23.

Folkard, S. (1983) Circadian rhythms and hours of work. In Warr, P. (ed.) *Psychology at Work*. Harmondsworth: Penguin.

Folkard, S. (1996) Bags of time to play. *Daily Express*, 28 September.

Freud, S. (1900) *The Interpretation of Dreams*. Republished in the Pelican Freud Library, vol. 4. Harmondsworth: Penguin, 1976.

Freud, S. (1901) The psychopathology of everyday life. Republished in Strachey, J. (ed.) *The Standard Edition of the Complete Psychological Works of Sigmund Freud*, vol. 6. London: Hogarth Press.

Freud, S. (1933) *New Introductory Lectures on Psychoanalysis*. London: Hogarth Press.

Gackenbach, J.I. (1994) Manifest content analysis of sleep laboratory collected lucid and non-lucid dreams. www.sawka.com/spirit-watch/manifest/htm

Gackenbach, J.I. and LaBerge, S. (eds) (1988) *Conscious Mind, Sleeping Brain: Perspectives on lucid dreaming*. New York: Plenum.

Gazzaniga, M.S. and Sperry, R.W. (1967) Language after section of the cerebral commisures. *Brain* 90, 131–48.

Gibson, H.B. and Heap, M. (1991) *Hypnosis in Therapy*. Hove: LEA.

Gold, D.R., Rogacz, S., Bock, N. *et al.* (1992) Rotating shift-work, sleep and accidents related to sleepiness in hospital nurses. *American Journal of Public Health* 82, 1011–14.

Gordon, N.P. (1986) The prevalence and health impact of shiftwork. *American Journal of Public Health* 76, 1225–8.

Green, S. (1998) Sleeping. *Psychology Review* 4 (3), February.

Gregory, R. and Zangwill, O.L. (1987) *The Oxford Companion to the Mind*. London: Oxford University Press.

Gribbin, M. (1990) All in a night's sleep. *New Scientist: Inside Science* 36, 7 July, http://www.newscientist.com/

Gruzelier, J.H. (1998) A working model of the neurophysiology of hypnosis: A review of evidence. *Contemporary Hypnosis* 15, 5.

Gulevich, G., Dement, W.C. and Johnson, L. (1966) Psychiatric and EEG observations on a case of prolonged (264 hours) wakefulness. *Archives of General Psychiatry* 15, 29–35.

Hart, C. and Hart, B.B. (1996) The use of hypnosis with children and adolescents. *The Psychologist* 9, 506–9.

Hawkins, L.H. and Armstrong-Esther, C.A. (1978) Circadian rhythms and night-shift working in nurses. *Nursing Times* 4 May, 49–52.

Hayes, N. (1994) *Foundations of Psychology*. London: Routledge. Second edition.

Hearne, K. (1980) Sleep: Insight into lucid dreams. *Nursing Mirror* 150 (10), 20–2.

Highfield, R. (1996) Scientists shed light on the origins of our body clock. *Daily Telegraph* 5 May.

Hilgard, E.R. (1975) Hypnosis. *Annual Review of Psychology* 26, 19–44.

Hilgard, E.R. (1977) Towards a neodissociationist theory: Multiple cognitive controls in human functioning. *Perspectives in Biology and Medicine* 17, 301–16.

Hilgard, J.R. (1979) *Personality and Hypnosis: A study of imaginative involvement*. Chicago: University of Chicago Press. Second edition, pp. 237–49.

Hobson, J.A. (1989) *Sleep*. New York: Scientific American Library.

Hobson, J.A. (1995) Sleeping and dreaming. In Kimbly, D. and Colman, A.M. (eds) *Biological Aspects of Behaviour*. London: Longman.

Hobson, J.A. and McCarley, R.W. (1977) The brain as a dream state generator: An activation–synthesis hypothesis of the dream process. *American Journal of Psychiatry* 134, 121.

Holmes, R. (ed.) (1997) *Night Moves: Mind Travellers, unravelling the mysteries of sleep. New Scientist* supplement, 26 April, 8–13.

Hopfield, J.J. (1984) Neurons with graded response have collective computational properties like those of two-state neurons. *Proceedings of the National Academy of Sciences USA* 81 (10), 3088–92.

Horne, J. (1988) *Why We Sleep: The functions of sleep in humans and other mammals*. Oxford: Oxford University Press.

Horne, J. (1992) Stay awake, stay alive. *New Scientist*, 4 January, http://www.newscientist.com/

Horne, J. and Minard, A. (1985) Sleep and sleepiness following a behaviourally 'active' day. *Ergonomics* 28, 567–75.

Huber-Weidman, H. (1976) *Sleep, Sleep Disturbances and Sleep Deprivation*. Cologne: Kiepenheuser and Witsch.

Jacobson, A. and Kales, A. (1967) Somnambulism: All-night EEG and related studies. In Kety, S.S., Evarts, E.V. and Williams, H.L. (eds) *Sleep and Altered States of Consciousness*. Baltimore: Williams and Wilkins.

James, W. (1890) *Principles of Psychology*. New York: Holt.

Jemmott, J.B., III, Borysenko, M., McCleland, D.C., Chapman, R., Meyer, D. and Benson, H. (1985) Academic stress, power motivation and decrease in salivary secretory immunoglobulin: A secretion rate. *Lancet* 1, 1400–2.

Jennet, B. and Plum, F. (1972) Persistent vegetative state after brain damage: A syndrome in search of a name. *Lancet* i, 734–7.

Jouvet, M. (1967) Mechanisms of the states of sleep: A neuropharmacological approach. *Research Publications of the Association for the Research in Nervous and Mental Diseases* 45, 86–126.

Kirsch, I. (1997) Suggestibility or hypnosis: what do our scales really measure? *The International Journal of Clinical and Experimental Hypnosis* 45, 212.

Kirsch, I. (1998) Dissociating the wheat from the chaff in theories of hypnosis: Reply to Kihlstrom. *Psychological Bulletins* 123 (2), 198–202.

Klein, R. and Armitage, R. (1979) Rhythms in human performance: 1.5 hour oscillations in cognitive style. *Science* 204, 1326–7.

Kleitman, N. (1963) *Sleep and Wakefulness*. Chicago: Chicago University Press. Revised and enlarged edition.

Kline, P. (1994) Some psychoanalytic perspectives. *Psychology Review* 1 (2), 7–9.

LaBerge, S. (1985) Lucid dreaming: Lucidity research, past and future. *Night Light* 5 (3), Fall, 1993. The Lucidity Institute.

Lamm, R.W. (1994) Morning light therapy for winter depression: Predictors of response. *Acta Psychiatria Scandinavia*.

Levine, M.E., Milliron, A.N. and Duffy, L.K. (1994) Diurnal and seasonal rhythms of melatonin, cortisol and testosterone in interior Alaska. *Arctic Medical Research* 53 (1), 25–34.

Lloyd, P., Mayes, A., Manstead, A.S.R., Mendell, P.R. and Wagner, H.L. (1984) *Introduction to psychology: An integrated approach*. London: Fontana.

Loftus, E.F. (1997) Creating false memories. *Scientific American*. September, 50–5.

Luce, G.G. (1971) *Body Time: Physiological rhythms and social stress*. New York: Pantheon.

Lugaresi, E., Medoru, R., Montagna, P., Baruzzi, A., Cortelli, P., Lugaresi, A., Tinuper, P., Zucconi, M. and Gambetti, P. (1986) Fatal familial insomnia and dysautonomia with selective degeneration of the thalamic nuclei. *New England Journal of Medicine* 315, 997–1003.

McClintock, M.K. (1971) Menstrual synchrony and suppression. *Nature* 229 (5282), 244–5.

McIlveen, R. (1995) Hypnosis. *Psychology Review* 2 (2), 8–12.

Maurice, D. (1998) The Von Sallmann Lecture 1996: An opthalmological explanation of REM sleep. *Experimental Eye Research* 66 (2), 139–45.

Meddis, R. (1975) On the function of sleep. *Animal Behaviour* 23, 676–91.

Meddis, R. (1977) *The Sleep Instinct*. London: Routledge and Kegan Paul.

Meddis, R. (1979) The evolution and function of sleep. In Oakley, D.A. and Plotkin, H.C. (eds) *Brain, Behaviour and Evolution*. London: Methuen.

Miles, L.E.M., Raynal, D.M. and Wilson, M.A. (1977) Blind man living in normal society has circadian rhythms of 24.9 hours. *Science* 198, 421–3.

Miller, R.J., Hennessy, R.T. and Leibowitz, H.W. (1973) The effect of hypnotic ablation of the background on the magnitude of the Ponzo perspective illusion. *International Journal of Clinical and Experimental Hypnosis* 21, 180–91.

Morgan, E. (1995) Measuring time with a biological clock. *Biological Sciences Review* 7, 2–5.

Mukhametov, L.M. (1984) Sleep in marine mammals. In Borbely, A.A. and Valatx, J.L. (eds) *Sleep Mechanisms*. Munich: Springer.

Novak, R.D., Smolensky, M.H., Fairchild, E.J. and Reves, R.R. (1990) Shiftwork and industrial injuries at a chemical plant in southeast Texas. *Chronobiology International* 7, 155–64.

Oakley, D.A. (1985) The plurality of consciousness, in Oakley, D.A.(ed.) *Brain and Mind*. London: Methuen.

Ornstein, R. (1986) *The Psychology of Consciousness*. Harmondsworth: Penguin. Revised second edition.

Oswald, I. (1970) *Sleep*. Harmondsworth: Penguin.

Oswald, I. (1976) The function of sleep. *Postgraduate Medical Journal* 52 (603), 15–18.

Oswald, I. (1980) Sleep as a restorative process: Human clues. *Progress in Brain Research* 53, 279–88.

Oswald, I. and Adam, K. (1980) The man who had not slept for ten years. *British Medical Journal* 281, 1684–5.

Palmer, J.D. (1989) Comparative studies of tidal rhythms: VIII. A translocation experiment involving circalunidian rhythms. *Marine Behaviour and Physiology* 14, 231–43.

Penfield, W. and Rasmussen, T. (1950) *The Cerebral Cortex of Man: A clinical study of localisation*. Boston: Little, Brown and Co.

Pengelley, E.T. and Fisher, K.C. (1957) Onset and cessation of hibernation under constant temperature and light in the golden-mantled ground squirrel, *Citellus lateralis. Nature* 180, 1371–2.

Perugini, E.M., Kirsch, I., Allen, S.T., Coldwell, E., Meredith, J.M. and Sheehan, J. (1998) Surreptitious observation of responses to hypnotically suggested hallucinations: A test of compliance hypothesis. *International Journal of Clinical Hypnosis* 46 (2), 191–203.

Pilleri, G. (1979) The blind Indus dolphin, *Platanista indi. Endeavour* 3, 48–56.

Pinell, J.P.J. (1993) *Biopsychology*. Boston: Allyn and Bacon. Second edition.

Popper, K.R. (1969) *Conjectures and Refutations: The growth of scientific knowledge*. London: Routledge and Kegan Paul. Revised third edition.

Prentice, P. (1995) Dream analysis. *Psychology Review* 2 (1).

Rainville, P., Hofbauer, R.K., Paus, T., Duncan, G.H., Bushnell, M.C. and Price, D.D. (1999) Cerebral mechanisms of hypnotic induction and suggestion. *Journal of Cognitive Neuroscience* 11 (1), 110–25.

Ramm, P. (1979) The locus coeruleus, catecholamines and REM sleep: A critical review. *Behavioural and Neural Biology* 25, 415–18.

Rechtschaffen, A., Bergmann, B.M., Everson, C.A., Kushida, C.A. and Gilliland, M.A. (1989) Sleep deprivation in the rat: 1. Conceptual issues. *Sleep* 12, 1–4.

Roberts, M.B.V. (1982) *Biology: A functional approach*. Walton-on-Thames: Thomas Nelson and Sons. Third edition.

Rose, S. (1976) *The Conscious Brain*. Harmondsworth: Penguin.

Russell, M.J., Switz, G.M. and Thompson, K. (1980) Olfactory influences on the human menstrual cycle. *Pharmacology, Biochemistry and Behaviour* 13, 737–8.

Sakai, K. (1985) Anatomical and physiological basis of paradoxical sleep. In McGinty, D., Morrison, A., Drucker-Colin, R.R. and Parmeggiani, P.L. (eds) *Brain Mechanisms of Sleep*. New York: Spectrum.

Sarbin, T.R. and Slagle, R.W. (1972) Hypnosis in psychophysiological outcomes. In Fromm, E. and Shor, R.E. (eds) *Hypnosis: Research, developments and perspectives*. Chicago: Aldine-Atherton.

Schatzman, M. (1992) Freud: Who seduced whom? *New Scientist*, 21 March, http://www.newscientist.com/

Schatzman, M., Worsley, A. and Fenwick, P. (1988) Correspondence during Lucid Dreams between Dreamed and Actual Events. In Gackenbach, J.L. and LaBerge, S. (eds) *Conscious Mind, Sleeping Brain: Perspectives on lucid dreaming*. New York: Plenum.

Schwartz, W., Recht, L. and Lew, R. (1995) Three time zones and you're out. *New Scientist*, 29 October, http://www.newscientist.com/

Seligman, M.E.P. (1970) On the generality of the laws of learning. *Psychological Review* 77, 406–18.

Selye, H. (1956) *The Stress of Life*. New York: McGraw-Hill.

Shapiro, C.M., Bortz, R., Mitchell, D., Bartel, P. and Jooste, P. (1981) Slow-wave sleep: A recovery period after exercise. *Science* 214, 1253–4.

Silber, K. (1999) *The Physiological Basis of Behaviour: Neural and hormonal processes*. London and New York: Routledge.

Skinner, B.F. (1938) *Science and Behaviour*. New York: Macmillan.

Solomon, G.F. (1969) Emotions, stress, the CNS and immunity. *Annals of the New York Academy of Sciences* 164, 335–43.

Spanos, N.P. (1986) Hypnotic behaviour: A social–psychological interpretation of amnesia, analgesia and 'trance logic'. *The Behavioural and Brain Sciences* 9, 499–502.

Spanos, N.P. (1991) A sociocognitive approach to hypnosis. In Lynn, S.J. and Rhue, J.W. (eds) *Theories of Hypnosis: Current models and perspectives*. New York: Guilford.

Spiegel, D., Kosslyn, S. and Thompson, W. (1998) You are feeling very, very sleepy. In Concar, D. (ed.) *New Scientist: Planet Science*, Archive, 4 July, http://www.newscientist.com/

States, B. (1997) *Seeing in the Dark: Reflections on dreams and dreaming*. New Haven and London: Yale University Press.

Stern, W.C. and Morgane, P.J. (1974) Theoretical view of REM sleep function: Maintenance of catecholamine systems in the central nervous system. *Behavioural Biology* 11, 1–32.

Stewart, J. and Amir, S. (1998) Body clocks get tired and emotional. *New Scientist*, 21 November, http://www.newscientist.com/

Tart, C.T. (1969) *Altered States of Consciousness*. New York: Wiley.

Van Eeden, F.W. (1913) *A Study of Dreams*. http://www.lucidity.com/vanEeden.html

Vogel, G.W. (1975) A review of REM sleep deprivation. *Archives of General Psychiatry* 32, 749–61.

Wagstaff, G.F. (1981) *Hypnosis, Compliance and Belief*. Brighton: Harvester.

Wagstaff, G.F. (1995) Hypnosis. In Colman, A.M. (ed.) *Controversies in Psychology*. London: Longman.

Watson, J. (1913) Psychology from the standpoint of a behaviourist. *Psychological Review* 20, 158–77.

Webb, W.B. (1975) *Sleep: The gentle tyrant*. Englewood Cliffs: Prentice Hall.

Webb, W.B. and Bonnet, M.H. (1978) The sleep of 'morning' and 'evening' types. *Biological Psychology* 7 (1–2), 29–35.

Wundt, W. (1862) *Beiträge zur Theorie der Sinneswahrnehmung*. Leipzig: C.F. Winter.

Zimbardo, P., McDermott, M., Jansz, J. and Metaal, N. (1995) *Psychology: A European text*. London: HarperCollins.

Index